Branded

The Unique Baby Name Book

By: Tonya L. Griffin

Order this book online at www.trafford.com
or email orders@trafford.com

Most Trafford titles are also available at major online book retailers.

Printed in Victoria, BC, Canada.

ISBN: 978-1-4269-2199-5 (sc)

Library of Congress Control Number: 2009912628

*Our mission is to efficiently provide the world's finest, most comprehensive book publishing
service, enabling every author to experience success. To find out how to publish your book, your
way, and have it available worldwide, visit us online at www.trafford.com*

Trafford rev. 11/18/2009

 www.trafford.com

North America & international
toll-free: 1 888 232 4444 (USA & Canada)
phone: 250 383 6864 ♦ fax: 812 355 4082

Girls

A

AALIYAH
AAMORI
AARI
AARIC
AARIKA
AARIONNE
ABBA
ABBIE
ABB
ABELLA
ABEN
ABENA
ABERY
ABIA
ABIGAIL
ABILENE
ABIRA
ABRASHA
ABRE
ABREY
ABRIANA
ABRIELLE
ABRIL
ACADIA
ACALENA
ACATIA
ACKALIN
ACKER
ACREE
ADAH
ADAIR
ADALIA
ADALIE

ADALIND
ADANNA
ADARA
ADDISON
ADDYSON
ADECYN
ADEEN
ADELA
ADELAIDE
ADELINE
ADELITA
ADELLE
ADELPHA
ADENA
ADERYN
ADESSA
ADILYNN
ADIRA
ADISA
ADORA
ADRA
ADRIANA
ADRIEL
ADRIENNE
ADYN
AELLY
AEREALE
AERENA
AEYON
AFINITY
AFRA
AFTON
AGATHA
AGATAA
AGENTINA
AGGIE
AGNES

AIDA
AIKEN
AILEEN
AILEY
AIMEE
AIMER
AINDA
AINSLEY
AISHA
AISLIM
AISLING
AISLINN
AKREN
AKSEL
ALAINA
ALALA
ALANDRA
ALANIS
ALASON
ALATHENA
ALBA
ALBIE
ALBINA
ALDONNA
ALDYS
ALEARA
ALEC
ALEDA
ALEENA
ALEGRA
ALEGRIA
ALEKSEY
ALENCIA
ALERA
ALESIA
ALESSA
ALETA

ALEXCIA
ALEXI
ALEXIS
ALICIA
ALIEGH
ALINA
ALISA
ALISE
ALIZA
ALLERTON
ALLEY
ALLIE
ALLISTER
ALLURA
ALLYE
ALLYN
ALLYNA
ALLYX
ALONA
ALONNA
ALORA
ALOUETTE
ALPHA
ALSTONIA
ALTHEA
ALTHENA
ALVES
ALVITA
ALYS
ALYSCHA
AMADA
AMALINA
AMALITA
AMANDRA
AMARA
AMARI
AMARIS

AMBER
AMBERLY
AMBRA
AMBREE
AMBRERRA
AMBRIELLE
AMBRIN
AMBROISE
AMBROSIA
AMEERAH
AMELIA
AMERICUS
AMES
AMINA
AMIRA
AMITY
AMIYA
AMORA
AMORELL
AMORITA
AMORY
AMRYKA
ANABELLA
ANABELLE
ANABRIL
ANALY
ANASTASIA
ANATOLA
ANAYSIS
ANCHOR
ANDA
ANDER
ANDERS
ANES
ANDRA
ANDREA
ANDREAN

ANDREE
ANDRENNA
ANDRIA
ANEKA
ANGE
ANGEL
ANGELINA
ANGLIN
ANITA
ANIYA
ANNALYNNE
ANNISA
ANNISE
ANNISTON
ANNUAL
ANONA
ANORA
ANSEL
ANSLEY
ANSOM
ANTHE
ANTOINETTE
ANTONELLE
ANWEN
ANYA
APOLLA
APPLE
APTHA
AQUA
AQUAN
ARA
ARABELLE
ARABI
ARAXIE
ARBELA
ARBOR
ARBOUR

ARBRA	ARY	AUDRA
ARBRAN	ARYA	AUDRAN
ARCELLE	ARYN	AUDREA
ARCH	ASH	AUDREY
ARDEN	ASHA	AUDRINA
ARDERY	ASHBY	AUGUSTA
ARDIANA	ASHE	AUGUSTINE
ARDRA	ASHER	AULIE
ARDYSS	ASHES	AUNDRA
ARENDYL	ASHLAND	AURA
ARETTA	ASHLIN	AURELIA
ARI	ASHLYN	AURELLA
ARIA	ASHNA	AURIAN
ARIANA	ASHTON	AURIEL
ARIANDA	ASHTYN	AURORA
ARIANNA	ASLERA	AURY
ARIANNE	ASPEN	AUSTINE
ARICA	ASRA	AUSTYN
ARIE	ASTA	AUTRA
ARIEL	ASTAR	AUTUMN
ARIES	ASTOR	AVA
ARIL	ASTORIA	AVALON
ARIONA	ASTRID	AVDIS
ARIS	ATARA	AVEN
ARIZONA	ATHENA	AVENA
ARLEANA	ATHIE	AVERIL
ARLEN	ATIA	AVERY
ARLYN	ATIANNA	AVERYLLE
ARYLYNNE	ATLEY	AVI
ARMANDA	ATRA	AVIANA
ARMANI	ATTILLA	AVIE
ARMENTA	AUBER	AVION
ARNICA	AUBIN	AVIS
ARNYX	AUBREY	AVITOR
AROSA	AUDEN	AVNER
ARRABELLA	AUDIA	AVON
ARRISSA	AUDIE	AVONIA

AVREN
AVRIL
AVRIT
AWEN
AXI
AXY
AYA
AYDA
AYENA
AYLIN
AYNONA
AYRA
AZLYNN
AZMON
AZRIELLE
AZURA

B

BAER
BAHIRA
BAILEY
BAILOR
BAILYN
BAIRD
BALAN
BALDREE
BALEDIN
BALLAD
BALLARD
BALSAM
BALYN
BANDER
BANDERS
BANDY
BANE
BANITA
BANKS
BANKSTON
BANNER
BANNING
BANSON
BAREND
BARICK
BARK
BARKER
BARLEY
BARNER
BARR
BARRAGON
BARRON
BARTH

BASEY
BASIA
BATES
BAYDEN
BAYER
BAYES
BAYLEE
BAYLOR
BAYNES
BAYONNE
BAYS
BAYSE
BEAGON
BEALE
BEATY
BECCA
BEILA
BELANN
BELEM
BELEN
BELIA
BELLA
BELLAMY
BELLE
BELLONA
BENECIA
BENN
BENNETT
BENNEY
BENNY
BENTLEY
BEORNA
BERG
BERE
BERGER
BERIT
BERKE

BERKLEY
BERKS
BERLIN
BERLYN
BERTRAN
BERTREN
BERWYN
BERYL
BESS
BETA
BETHAMIE
BETHANNY
BETHANY
BETTA
BEULAH
BEVIL
BEYONCE
BIAN
BIANCA
BIBI
BICE
BILLINGS
BILSON
BINALI
BINDEN
BIONA
BIRCH
BIRGER
BIRGITTE
BIRKETT
BIRKEY
BISHOP
BITTA
BIVAN
BIVONA
BLAINE
BLAINEN

BLAINIE	BORDEN	BRIALLEN
BLAIR	BOSTON	BRIANNE
BLAISE	BOUREY	BRIAR
BLAKE	BOWIE	BRIDE
BLAKELY	BRACYLYN	BRIDEL
BLANCA	BRADIA	BRIDGES
BLANCHE	BRAELEE	BRIE
BLANDA	BRAILEY	BRIELLA
BLANTON	BRAISLY	BRIELYN
BLAZE	BRAISON	BRIERS
BLEDDYN	BRALYN	BRIGHTON
BLEN	BRAMBLE	BRILEY
BLEND	BRAMLETT	BRINKS
BLENDA	BRANAGEN	BRINSLEY
BLESS	BRANCH	BRINSON
BLESSING	BRANCHES	BRISTYL
BLEU	BRANTEN	BRISTYN
BLISS	BRANWEN	BRITT
BLODWEN	BRASON	BRITAIN
BLOSSOM	BRATUM	BRITANNY
BLUM	BRAXLYN	BRITON
BLUSH	BRAYAH	BRITTON
BLY	BRAYDIA	BRONWYN
BLYDE	BREA	BROOKEL
BLYTHE	BREANE	BROOKINGS
BO	BRECK	BROOKLYN
BOANAN	BRECKIN	BROOKS
BOBBIERRAE	BREENA	BRUMLEY
BOISE	BREESE	BRUSH
BOLA	BRELAND	BRYA
BOLTON	BRENGTH	BRYANY
BONETT	BRENLEY	BRYCE
BONILLE	BRENNA	BRYCY
BONITA	BRENTLEY	BRYE
BONNETT	BRETLON	BRYELLYN
BOOTS	BRI	BRYER
BORA	BRIA	BRYERS

BRYLEE
BRYLER
BRYLEY
BRYN
BRYNDI
BRYNLEE
BRYNNA
BRYNSLEY
BRYNSON
BRYNTHE
BRYXSON
BURCH
BURCHER
BURCHESS
BURDELLA
BURDELLE
BURKE
BURKES
BURLIEGH
BURNELLA
BURNELLE
BURNS
BYRIA
BYTHIA

C

	CAPTAIN	CATALINA
	CARA	CATALYNA
	CARALYN	CATRICE
	CARDEN	CAULIN
CABOT	CAREENA	CADENCE
CABRERA	CARIANNE	CAYEEN
CACYN	CARINA	CEARA
CADALYN	CARINE	CECELIA
CAELYN	CARISSA	CEETA
CAGNEY	CARLANDA	CELES
CALENDA	CARLEE	CELESTE
CALHOUN	CARLEY	CELESTIA
CALIA	CARLI	CELIA
CALINA	CARLIE	CELINA
CALISE	CARMEL	CELINE
CALISTA	CARMEN	CELLESTE
CALIXSTA	CARMIELA	CELSEY
CALLIE	CARNEA	CELSIA
CALLIOPE	CARNES	CEMBER
CALLY	CARNEY	CERA
CALM	CARNIE	CERELIA
CALYSTA	CAROLINE	CERENA
CAMBRELL	CARRELLE	CERINA
CAMBRIA	CARRIGON	CERISE
CAMERON	CARRINGTON	CESARY
CAMI	CARSLEY	CHABISE
CAMILLE	CARSTEN	CHAFIN
CAIYAH	CARSTINE	CHAHNA
CAMMIE	CARYA	CHAKA
CAMORA	CARYNE	CHALEE
CAMRYN	CARYNIESE	CHALEY
CANARY	CARYS	CHALINA
CANDELARA	CASLYNN	CHAMAYNE
CANDER	CASS	CHAMBRY
CANDICE	CASSIA	CHANA
CANDRA	CASSIDY	CHANDI
CANTERA	CASYN	CHANDLE

CHANDRA	CHRISTAN	CLOE
CHANDRIA	CHRISTIAN	CLOI
CHANEL	CHUTNEY	CLOREY
CHANIA	CHYNTEL	CLORINDA
CHANIEL	CIAN	CLOUD
CHANNER	CIANDRA	CLOVE
CHANNING	CIANNA	CLOVER
CHANTILL	CIARA	CLOVES
CHAPIN	CICELY	CLYN
CHARDE	CICILLIA	CLYSTIA
CHARELLE	CIDNE	COCO
CHARISS	CIMMERSON	COFFEY
CHARLESE	CINAMON	COIYA
CHARLEY	CINDER	COLERE
CHARLISE	CIONA	COLETTA
CHARLIZE	CIRI	COLETTE
CHARLYN	CLAIRA	COLINA
CHARLYSA	CLAIRE	COLINE
CHARMAINE	CLANEY	COLISA
CHARNA	CLARA	COLLENA
CHARNESS	CLARALYN	COLLIE
CHAYAN	CLARICE	COLYNNE
CHELENE	CLARIE	COLYX
CHELSEA	CLARINDA	CONCEPCION
CHELSEY	CLARINNE	CONCETTA
CHENILLE	CLARIS	CONENE
CHENSYN	CLARITY	CONESA
CHENTAL	CLARISSE	CONLEE
CHESLEY	CLARYSE	CONNER
CHESNEY	CLASSIE	CONNERY
CHESTLEY	CLAUDETTE	CONSTANCE
CHEYENNE	CLAUDIA	CONSTATINE
CHINA	CLEANDRA	CONSUELA
CHORA	CLEARA	CONSUELO
CHORDE	CLEO	CONTESSA
CHORDEN	CLETHA	CONTINA
CHRISMA	CLISTA	COPELAND

CORAL	CROFT
CORALINE	CRYLER
CORANCA	CULLEN
CORD	CURI
CORDELIA	CURINE
CORDELINA	CURSTEN
CORDULA	CYAN
CORETTE	CYANN
CORI	CYDNEY
CORIANDER	CYLEE
CORIANNE	CYLENE
CORINE	CYLER
CORINNA	CYLIA
CORINTHA	CYNARA
CORLISS	CYNDER
CORLYN	CYNTRILLE
CORRINA	CYPRESS
CORVINA	CYRA
COSTNER	CYRI
COUMEL	CYRILLA
COURDAY	CZARA
COURTNEY	CZAREE
COVIN	CZARINA
COYAH	
CRAFT	
CRANDELL	
CREASON	
CREED	
CREIGHTON	
CREST	
CRESTON	
CRICKETT	
CRIMSON	
CRISELLE	
CRISPIN	
CRISTA	
CRITTEN	

D

DACEY
DAELEN
DAGNEY
DAHLIA
DAHRI
DAI
DAISHA
DAISY
DAITON
DAKOTA
DALYNA
DALYNE
DALENA
DALL
DALYNA
DAMARA
DAMARIS
DAMONE
DANE
DANALA
DANALE
DANCER
DANEA
DANEEN
DANENA
DANESSA
DANEY
DANI
DANICA
DANIELLA
DANIELLE
DANIR
DANNA

DANNER
DANTE
DARA
DARBRY
DARBY
DARCI
DARCY
DARI
DARLA
DARLEE
DARMA
DAROLYN
DARSHA
DARVA
DARVY
DARYNA
DASHAWN
DASMINE
DASSIA
DAVIE
DAVINA
DAYBREE
DAYLA
DAYSHA
DAYTEN
DAYTON
DAZZLE
DAZZLYN
DEACON
DEANA
DEANNA
DEATRA
DEBIENE
DECCAN
DECLARE
DEIDRA
DEJA

DELANIE
DELAYNA
DELIA
DELILAH
DELINA
DELLA
DELLANA
DELLIA
DELLORA
DELORA
DELPHINA
DELSA
DELTA
DELYNN
DEMI
DENALI
DENDA
DENEDRA
DENI
DENILLE
DENIM
DENNIE
DENOVIA
DERA
DERBY
DERYN
DESA
DESAI
DESENA
DESIREE
DESLA
DESLIN
DESTANY
DESTINY
DESTRY
DETRA
DEVA

DEVERA	DODIE	DRURY
DEVI	DOHERTY	DRUSILLA
DEVINA	DOLAH	DUCHESS
DEVYNE	DOLLIS	DUENA
DHANI	DOLLY	DUFF
DHARA	DOLORY	DUFFY
DHARMA	DOMINIQUE	DUNA
DHESSIE	DONNATE	DUPRE
DHIRA	DORA	DUPREE
DHIVIA	DORANNE	DURRANN
DIA	DORETHA	DURREN
DIAMOND	DORI	DUSKY
DIAMONTE	DORIA	DUSTIE
DIANDRA	DORIAN	DUSTINE
DIANMANTE	DORIN	DUSTY
DIEDRE	DORINA	DWYLA
DILIA	DORITA	DYAN
DILLARD	DORY	DYANDRA
DIMON	DOTT	DYLANA
DINAH	DOTTIE	DYME
DINAVIA	DOVE	DYMOND
DINORA	DOVIE	DYNASTY
DINORAH	DOXIE	DYONNE
DIOMA	DRAKE	DYSON
DION	DRAVEN	
DIONNE	DRAYLYN	
DIOR	DREA	
DITA	DREAM	
DIVA	DREAMA	
DIVERSITY	DREAMER	
DIVINA	DRENDA	
DIVINE	DRENNA	
DIVINITY	DRIANA	
DIVORA	DRISENA	
DIXIE	DRISENDA	
DIYA	DRIVER	
DOCILLE	DRUELLA	

E

EADIE
EADY
EAGAN
EAMES
EADMON
EARLY
EASLYN
EASTER
EASTERN
EASTON
EAVAN
EAVIE
EBBA
EBBIE
EBELLA
EBEN
EBONY
EBREL
ECHO
ECKLEY
EDA
EDDA
EDDYE
EDEN
EDESSA
EDIE
EDINA
EDITH
EDLYN
EDONA
EDRICA
EDYTHE
EFFEN

EFFIE
EGAN
EGYPT
EILEEN
EIRES
EIVES
ELANA
ELANAH
ELANI
ELARA
ELBA
ELEANOR
ELECTRA
ELEDA
ELEKTRA
ELENI
ELETTRA
ELEXIS
ELI
ELIANA
ELISA
ELISE
ELITE
ELIZA
ELKE
ELKES
ELLA
ELLAGRACE
ELLE
ELLEGANCE
ELLEN
ELLERY
ELLESA
ELLIAN
ELLIANCE
ELLICE
ELLIE

ELLINA
ELLINGTON
ELLISA
ELM
ELONA
ELORA
ELSA
ELSBETH
ELSKE
ELVA
ELVEETRA
ELVINA
ELVIRA
ELYSSA
ELYSSE
EMANI
EMANN
EMBER
EME
EMELIA
EMENY
EMERA
EMERALD
EMERY
EMILEE
EMILY
EMILYN
EMINA
EMIRA
EMITY
EMLYN
EMMANUEL
EMME
EMMIE
EMMY
EMPIRA
ENDA

ENERGY   ETHINA
ENGLAND   ETHNE
ENGRAM   ETTA
ENNA   EUDORA
ENORA   EULA
ENVI   EULALA
ENVY   EULANDA
ENYA   EUSTACIA
EPIC   EUVENIA
EPLEY   EVA
ERA   EVALINA
ERCELLA   EVALINE
ERDELL   EVANGELIA
ERES   EVANGELINA
ERIN   EVANNA
ERINA   EVELINA
ERINDA   EVER
ERLYNN   EVERS
ERLYNNE   EVERY
ERONA   EVEY
ERYNE   EVIE
ESHA   EVINE
ESNE   EVITA
ESPY   EVONNE
ESRA   EWING
ESSENCE   EYDIA
ESSIE   EZRA
ESTA
ESTALYN
ESTANA
ESTEE
ESTELLA
ESTELLE
ESTH
ESTINE
ETERNITY
ETHELEN

F

FACEN
FACTOR
FADEN
FAEL
FAGEN
FAGON
FAGYN
FAINES
FAIRON
FAITH
FAITHE
FALLEN
FALLES
FALLIN
FALLON
FALYNN
FAMBER
FANCY
FANNING
FANNON
FANTINE
FARINA
FARIS
FARLEY
FARRAH
FARREN
FARROW
FARY
FASHION
FATHOM
FAULK
FAWN
FAXON

FAYLA
FEARCE
FEARS
FEATHER
FEDORA
FELICITY
FELISE
FELYN
FENA
FENIA
FENNELLE
FENWICH
FERGI
FERGUSON
FERNAND
FEY
FIDELA
FIDELITY
FIELDS
FIERSTON
FIFER
FINA
FINES
FINLEY
FINNESSE
FION
FIONA
FIRESTON
FLAIR
FLAME
FLANNERY
FLAVINE
FLINT
FLO
FLOR
FLORENS
FLORENT

FLORINA
FLORRIE
FLORRY
FLOSSIE
FLOWER
FLOWERS
FLYNN
FOLA
FOLKE
FONDA
FONICE
FONTAINE
FONTINE
FORTUNE
FOWLER
FRA
FRAILE
FRANCE
FRANCES
FRANCESCA
FRANCHESCA
FRANCHINA
FRANCINE
FRANKIE
FRANN
FRANNIE
FREA
FREN
FRENCHIE
FRESSIA
FRISTEEL
FULLER
FURY
FUSCHIA
FYNDOM

G

GABBIE
GABBRIELLE
GABLE
GABRIELLA
GACEY
GACILYA
GAILYN
GAINES
GAITWYN
GALA
GALENA
GALIANA
GALISE
GAMIN
GAN
GANDY
GARLAND
GARLENE
GARLIN
GARMAN
GARMOND
GARNET
GARVEY
GATES
GAVIE
GAVOTTE
GAVRIELLA
GAYA
GEAH
GEDERAH
GEM
GEMMA
GEMS

GEN
GENA
GENAY
GENAYA
GENELL
GENELLA
GENERA
GENEVIEVE
GENNA
GENOA
GENOVA
GENTLE
GENTRY
GENZ
GEOMA
GEONNA
GEORGIA
GERMAINE
GERRI
GESS
GEYA
GEZELLE
GEZZIE
GHEA
GHERLAND
GHISTAINE
GHITA
GIA
GIANELLE
GIANI
GIANNA
GIBBON
GIBBONS
GILI
GILLIAN
GILLIS
GINAE

GINGER
GIORDANNA
GIOVANNA
GISELLA
GISELLE
GITANA
GIVA
GIVEN
GIVENS
GLADDEN
GLADE
GLAM
GLAMOUR
GLASS
GLEAM
GLEE
GLENDORA
GLENDYL
GLENNA
GLENNICE
GLENYS
GLORI
GLORIELLE
GLORIS
GLOW
GLYNIS
GLYNN
GOLDEN
GOLDIE
GOLDIN
GOLDO
GORGIE
GRACE
GRACEANNE
GRACELAND
GRACIA
GRACIE

GRACIELA
GRACLY
GRACYN
GRAFTON
GRAIL
GRAINE
GRAINNE
GRANA
GRANADA
GRATIA
GRAVE
GRAVES
GRAYDYN
GRAYLEY
GRAYLYN
GRAYSHA
GRAZIE
GREELEY
GRETA
GRETCHEN
GRETTA
GREYLAND
GRICE
GRICIE
GRICYN
GRIFFIN
GRINDELL
GRINER
GRISELDA
GRISHAM
GROVE
GUARD
GUARDS
GUENNA
GUESSA
GURLENE
GUSKIE

GUSSIE
GWEN
GWENDA
GWENLIN
GWENNA
GWYNETH
GWYNLYN
GYDA
GYLLA
GYNETTE
GYPSY
GYSELLE

H

HADLEE
HADLEY
HADWEN
HADY
HAGEN
HAGRID
HAINES
HALDA
HALDEN
HALDI
HALEN
HALENE
HALEY
HALIA
HALINA
HALLA
HALLE
HALLES
HALLIE
HALO
HALSEY
HAMMIE
HAMPTON
HANDERS
HANIGAN
HANNAH
HANNIAH
HANNIE
HANSON
HARA
HARBIN
HARBOR
HARBOUR

HARKEN
HARLA
HARLAND
HARLENA
HARLEY
HARLI
HARLOW
HARMON
HARMONY
HARNE
HARNES
HAROLYN
HARPE
HARRAH
HARRIET
HARRINGTON
HARRISAH
HARTIGAN
HARTLEY
HARUM
HARVARD
HATŠY
HATTIE
HAVA
HAVANA
HAVANAH
HAVEN
HAYDEN
HAYDYN
HAYES
HALEY
HAYLOW
HAYLYN
HAZAEL
HAZE
HAZEL
HAZELTON

HAZEN
HEALEY
HEALY
HEARST
HEART
HEATH
HEAVEN
HEELEY
HEIDI
HEISLEY
HELA
HELAINE
HELANNA
HELAYNE
HELENA
HELENE
HELGA
HELIE
HELLER
HELMS
HELSA
HELSEY
HENDA
HENDER
HENDLEY
HENIA
HENLEY
HENNAH
HENSLEY
HENTON
HERA
HERIAN
HERRA
HERRIN
HERRING
HERSALA
HIEVEN

HIAH	HOSANNA
HIATT	HOUSTON
HIDEE	HUATT
HIDIE	HUDSON
HIERS	HUELLA
HILDA	HUETTE
HILLERY	HULDA
HILLES	HUMBER
HILLARD	HUNNIE
HILTON	HURLEY
HINA	HURLIE
HINDA	HUTTON
HINDAL	HYACINTH
HINDER	HYDEN
HINES	HYDIA
HINTON	
HOLBROOK	
HOLDEN	
HOLDER	
HOLIDAY	
HOLINE	
HOLLAND	
HOLLINS	
HOLLIS	
HOLLISHA	
HOLLYN	
HOLSEY	
HOLTEN	
HOLTON	
HOLYN	
HONESTY	
HONEY	
HONORA	
HONORIA	
HOPE	
HORIYA	
HORIZON	

I

IANA
IANANNA
IATOLLA
IBBIE
IBBY
IBETH
ISBEN
IDA
IDAHLIA
IDALIA
IDARAH
IDASIA
IDEH
IDELL
IDELLIA
IDES
IDIO
IDOL
IDOLA
IDOLINA
IDOLYNE
IDOMA
IDONA
IDONIE
IDONY
IDRA
IESHA
IESHIA
IKEA
IKEIDA
ILARI
ILARIA
ILEANA

ILENA
ILESHA
ILIA
ILLANA
ILON
ILONKA
ILYSE
ILYSSA
IMAERA
IMAGINE
IMAINE
IMALA
IMAN
IMANA
IMARA
IMARI
IMAYRA
IMENA
IMPERESS
IMPERIA
INDA
INDAH
INDER
INDIA
INDIANA
INDIE
INDIECE
INDIGO
IDRA
INDRANI
INDYA
INESSA
INETHA
INFINITY
INGALLS
INGLESA
INGRAD

INGRID
INNA
INNOCENSE
INO
INOLA
INSLEY
INTEGRITY
IOLA
IONA
IONICA
IPEK
IRELYND
IRETA
IRIE
IRINA
IRISAL
IRISH
IRLANDA
ISABEL
ISABELLA
ISADORA
ISELA
ISHA
ISHANA
ISHTAR
ISIS
ISLA
ISLEANA
ISMAELA
ISMAELDA
ISMENIA
ISOLA
ISOTTA
ISRA
ITALIA
ITICA
ITKA

IVA
IVERY
IVES
IVETTE
IVEY
IVIANNAH
IVIS
IVISSE
IVNIA
IVORIES
IVORY
IVRIA
IVRIE
IVY
IWONA
IYANA
IZABELLA
IZABELLE
IZANNE
IZENA
IZZIE
IZZY

J

JACALYN
JACENDA
JACEY
JACIE
JACINTA
JACLYN
JACQUEL
JACQUET
JADA
JADE
JADD
JADESSA
JADIE
JADINE
JADWIN
JAELA
JAENESHA
JAGEN
JAGGEN
JAIDON
JARYN
JAKAYLA
JAIRA
JALIAH
JALIYAH
JALONA
JAMICA
JAMEAH
JAMILA
JAMILLE
JANA
JANAE
JANALYN

JANARA
JANAY
JANAYA
JANDI
JANDY
JANEENE
JANEER
JANEL
JANELLA
JANELLE
JANESA
JANIA
JANIE
JANIECE
JANIS
JANISSE
JANIYAH
JANSEN
JANTZEN
JAPANA
JARDANA
JARDESCA
JARENDA
JARMILA
JARRAH
JASALINE
JASI
JASIE
JASIRA
JASMINE
JATUMN
JAVANA
JAVIERA
JAYA
JAYCI
JAYDEN
JAYDIE

JAYDRA
JAYE
JAYLA
JAYLEE
JAYLENA
JAYLENE
JAYLYNN
JAYMES
JAYNILLE
JAYSIA
JAZ
JAZZ
JEANA
JECELYN
JELANA
JELANI
JELENA
JEM
JEMMA
JENAE
JANAYA
JANEA
JENILLE
JENIS
JENNA
JENNALEE
JENNER
JENNINGS
JENNIS
JENNISON
JENSON
JENTRY
JENZ
JERDIN
JERETTA
JERSEY
JESARAE

JESARY	JOLEY	JUDGES
JESMIN	JOLIE	JUDITH
JESMINE	JONBENETTE	JUEL
JESS	JONES	JULA
JESSA	JONNA	JULES
JESSAMINE	JONTELLE	JULIA
JESSIE	JOPLIN	JULIAN
JESSIRAY	JORDAN	JULIANA
JETTA	JORDANNA	JULIE
JETTE	JORGEN	JULIET
JEWELL	JORIE	JULISSA
JIANNA	JORY	JULIZA
JILANA	JOSANY	JUNEA
JIMMIE	JOSCELIN	JUNIA
JISOLA	JOSETTA	JUNITH
JNAE	JOSETTE	JUNO
JO	JOSHLYN	JURGAN
JOANA	JOSIE	JUS
JOANIE	JOSLYN	JUSTICE
JOBI	JOSSALIN	JUSTILLE
JOCELLA	JOSTAN	JUSTINA
JOCELYN	JOSTIN	JUSTINE
JOCI	JOURNEY	JYDEN
JODIE	JOVANA	JYNEESA
JOELE	JOVANNAH	JYNEICE
JOELEE	JOVI	
JOELEY	JOY	
JOELI	JOYALLE	
JOELLE	JOYCELLA	
JOELY	JOYOUS	
JOHANNA	JOYSLYN	
JOI	JOZEL	
JOINER	JUBILEE	
JOLA	JUCINDA	
JOLAN	JUDE	
JOLENA	JUDEA	
JOLENE	JUDGE	

K

KACIE
KADENCE
KADIA
KADYN
KAELA
KAELAND
KAI
KAIDA
KAILEE
KAILEIGH
KAILING
KAILYNN
KAIMAN
KANINAN
KAIRA
KAISLEY
KATIYN
KALEA
KALENA
KALEY
KALI
KALIDA
KALIE
KALINDA
KALLIE
KALLISTA
KAMBRIE
KAMEE
KAMELIA
KAMEN
KAMIAH
KAMILLE
KAMMIE
KAMOYA

KAMREN
KAMRI
KANDA
KANDLE
KANDRA
KANDYL
KANLEE
KANNAH
KANNON
KANYON
KAPLAN
KARANA
KARINA
KARISSA
KARISTA
KARLEE
KARLEY
KARLIE
KARLIN
KARLYN
KARMA
KARMELL
KARELLA
KARMELLE
KARMEN
KARMILLA
KARMILLE
KARMYN
KARNA
KAROLINE
KARRE
KARRIGAN
KARSON
KARSTEN
KASSIDY
KAT
KATCHI

KATERA
KATO
KAYA
KAYDEE
KAYDELL
KAYE
KAYLEN
KAYLOR
KAYLYNN
KAYSE
KEA
KEALEY
KEANA
KEANAH
KEANAN
KEANE
KEANNE
KEATING
KEATLEY
KEATS
KEEANNE
KEEDERA
KEELAND
KEELEY
KEELING
KEEN
KEENA
KEENAN
KEENE
KEEPE
KEERAH
KEERSTAIN
KEETRA
KEGAN
KEIGH
KEIRAN
KEIRRA

KEIRSTEN	KERENSA	KILSON
KEIRSTI	KERSEN	KIMAN
KELAR	KERSEY	KIMBALL
KELBY	KERST	KIMBER
KELLEN	KERSTIN	KIMBRA
KELLER	KESSIE	KIBBRELL
KELLIE	KESTON	KIMBUR
KELLY	KEVA	KINCAID
KELLYN	KEY	KINDELL
KELSEY	KEYES	KINDER
KELSON	KEYLAR	KINDRED
KEMP	KHAI	KINDRIA
KEMPLEY	KHALI	KINLEY
KEMPTON	KHALIDA	KINNELL
KENA	KHASHA	KINSA
KENDON	KHLOE	KINSEY
KINDRA	KHORUS	KINSLEY
KENDRAH	KHYRA	KINZI
KENDRED	KI	KIONA
KENDRELL	KIA	KIPLER
KENDRICK	KIAN	KIPLING
KENDRINA	KIANA	KIRA
KENDRY	KIARA	KIRAN
KENDYL	KIELA	KIRKLAND
KENLEY	KIENNE	KIRKLEY
KENNA	KIERA	KIRKSEY
KENNALYN	KIERAN	KIRSTIE
KENNAN	KIERI	KIRSTIN
KENNDRA	KIERRA	KISHA
KENNEDY	KIERSTEN	KIT
KENNETY	KIESHA	KIWANIS
KENNISON	KILA	KLARA
KENSITAN	KILAINA	KLARISSA
KENTLEY	KILBOURN	KLARYBELL
KENYA	KILEY	KLAUDIA
KENZI	KILI	KLEE
KERA	KILLI	KLEIN

KLEMANS
KLEMENS
KLYRA
KNEELIE
KNOLLES
KNOWLES
KOHL
KOHLS
KONA
KONSTANCE
KORA
KORAL
KOREENA
KOREN
KORI
KORINA
KORNELIA
KORRIGEN
KORRINE
KORTNEY
KOSTA
KOYA
KRISHEN
KRISSA
KRISSEN
KRISTA
KRISTALL
KRISTIE
KRISTINA
KRISTINE
KRISTYN
KRYS
KRYSTA
KRYSTAL
KULLEN
KURARA
KURENE

KWANN
KWASI
KWYNN
KWYNTYN
KYA
KYAN
KYELLA
KYLA
KYLANA
KYLARA
KYLEE
KYLIE
KYNCI
KYNDRED
KYOTI
KYRA
KYREE
KYRIA

L

LACEY
LACHELLE
LACHLAN
LACI
LADEN
LADENNA
LADEY
LADYN
LAE
LAELA
LAGEN
LAINEY
LAITH
LAKE
LAKENY
LAKINA
LALAH
LALAN
LALANEY
LALENA
LALITA
LALITHA
LALLEY
LALLY
LANA
LANAI
LAND
LANDA
LANDERS
LANDES
LANDI
LANDRY
LANDY
LANEL

LANET
LANIE
LANIER
LANNA
LANNAH
LANNETTE
LANSING
LANTAINA
LANTANA
LANUAL
LARAE
LARAY
LAREINA
LARGO
LARISSA
LARK
LARKEN
LARKIN
LARNI
LARSE
LARSEN
LARYN
LARYSA
LATICE
LATINA
LATISA
LATRELLE
LAUER
LAUGHLIN
LAUNA
LAUNDA
LAURENA
LAURIE
LAURNA
LAURNALEE
LAVADA
LAVENA

LAVENDER
LAVERNE
LAVILLE
LAVINIE
LAXEY
LAYINE
LAYLA
LAYNN
LAYRE
LAYTON
LEA
LEAH
LEALA
LEANA
LEANDER
LEANDRA
LEANNE
LEANORA
LEDA
LEESY
LEGEND
LEGRA
LEI
LEIGHTON
LEILA
LEITH
LEIYA
LEJALLE
LELA
LENAE
LENAYA
LENDORA
LENICE
LENKAN
LENOX
LENTON
LENYE

LEODA	LILIAH	LOCKETT
LEOLA	LILITH	LOEN
LEOMA	LILLIAN	LOGAN
LEONA	LILLY	LOGANAH
LEONORA	LILY	LOGEN
LEORA	LINA	LOLA
LERA	LINDEN	LOLIA
LEREMY	LINDI	LOMA
LESLIE	LINDSEY	LONA
LETA	LINES	LONDA
LETHA	LINETTE	LONDON
LETINA	LINK	LONI
LETSEY	LINKES	LONICA
LETTIE	LIOTTA	LONNETTE
LEVANA	LISBET	LOPA
LEX	LISBETH	LORA
LEXA	LISETTE	LORAINE
LEXANNE	LITA	LORALEE
LEXIE	LITZY	LORANDE
LEXINE	LIV	LORDYN
LEXIS	LIVE	LOREL
LEXUS	LIVI	LORELEI
LEYDEN	LIVIA	LORELLE
LEZLEE	LIVIE	LOREN
LIA	LIVINIA	LORENA
LIANNA	LIVVY	LORI
LIBBY	LIZ	LORIANNE
LIBERTY	LIZA	LORNABETH
LIBIA	LIZELLE	LOVE
LIBRA	LIZETTE	LOVELLA
LIDDAN	LIZZIE	LOVINA
LIDELLE	LIZZY	LOWERY
LIDIA	LLANA	LOWRY
LIESE	LLEYTON	LOYAL
LIKEN	LOA	LUCIE
LIL	LOCKE	LUCILLA
LILAC	LOCKES	LUCINDA

LUDORA
LUELLA
LUNDA
LULANI
LUNAR
LUNDYN
LUNIA
LURA
LURISSA
LUX
LYANNA
LYANNE
LYDEA
LYDIA
LYNDSEY
LYNDYN
LYNELLE
LYNES
LYNETTE
LYNITA
LYNK
LYNN
LYNONA
LYRA
LYRIC
LYRIN
LYRIS
LYSA
LYSLE

M

MABEE
MABREY
MACAYLA
MACI
MACKENA
MACYN
MADALEN
MADDYE
MADELINE
MADGE
MADIA
MADISON
MADONNA
MADRID
MAESA
MAGNOLIA
MAIA
MAINE
MAIYA
MALAEA
MALAYA
MALAYNA
MALEA
MALEN
MALINDA
MALINN
MALLEY
MALLORY
MAMES
MAMIE
MANDA
MANDELY
MANICA

MAPLE
MARADON
MARCELE
MARCELLA
MARCELLE
MARCIER
MARDELLA
MARDEN
MARDEY
MARDI
MAREEL
MARENA
MARGO
MARGOT
MARIAH
MARIBEL
MARICATHERINE
MARIEL
MARIGOLD
MARINA
MARING
MARINNA
MARISKA
MARISOL
MARISOLE
MARISSA
MARKEY
MARLAE
MARLAINA
MARLEA
MARLENA
MARLENE
MARLETTE
MARLEY
MARLO
MARNA
MAROLYN

MARRA
MARRIBEL
MARRINER
MARSALE
MARSANNE
MARVADA
MARYANNE
MARYBAH
MARYBETH
MATEA
MAUSEY
MAVIN
MAVIS
MAWAN
MAXIE
MAYA
MAYBREY
MAYE
MAYES
MAYLEE
MAYLYNA
MAYLYNN
MAZIE
MCCALL
MCGEE
MCGRAY
MCKAIDEN
MCKAY
MCKEE
MCKENNA
MCKENSIE
MCKINLEY
MCKINNEY
MCLEAN
MCLEOD
MEADE
MEADOW

MEADOWS	MERYSSA	MIRUS
MEDALLA	MEYERS	MISCHA
MEDEA	MIA	MISTIQUE
MEDINA	MICAELA	MISTY
MEDLEY	MICAH	MITZI
MEG	MIKELLA	MIYA
MEGAN	MILA	MOBLEY
MELEAH	MILAN	MOETTA
MELEDA	MILANA	MOHANA
MELINA	MILANDA	MOLLY
MELINDA	MILANI	MONA
MELLIE	MILANIE	MONET
MELODY	MILAYNAH	MONIQUE
MELROSE	MILBANK	MONTANA
MENA	MILEE	MONTROSE
MENDEE	MILEY	MOON
MENDY	MILLAY	MORBAN
MENNA	MILLICANT	MORENA
MENTON	MILLIE	MORGAN
MERAE	MILLS	MORIAH
MERCEDES	MILNER	MORIE
MERCER	MIMI	MORIGAN
MERCHANT	MIMOSA	MORIN
MERCIA	MINA	MORLA
MERCY	MINCH	MORNA
MEREDITH	MINDY	MOSELLE
MEREDYTH	MINERVA	MOTIE
MERIT	MINOR	MOTTA
MERLEE	MINTER	MOXIE
MERRIBETH	MIRA	MULANIS
MERRIDY	MIRABELLA	MUNDY
MERRIDYN	MIRACLE	MURIEL
MERRIGAN	MIRAL	MURLIE
MERRITT	MIRANDA	MURPHY
MERRYNN	MIRELDA	MURRIEL
MERSEY	MIRELLA	MURTRY
MERYNDA	MIRIAM	MUSA

MYA
MYAN
MYANA
MYCA
MYDA
MYER
MYERS
MYISHA
MYKALA
MYLBANKS
MYLEE
MYLER
MYLIE
MYNDEL
MYNE
MYNOR
MYRA
MYRIAM
MYRISA
MYRNA
MYSHA
MYSTA
MYSTIC
MYSTIQUE
MYSTRY

N

NABOR
NACIE
NADARA
NADASEN
NADLINE
NADETTE
NADIA
NADINE
NADRIE
NADRINA
NAHARA
NAIDA
NAIJA
NAILAH
NAKIA
NALANI
NALANIE
NALYNN
NAMI
NAN
NANCE
NANI
NAOLA
NAOMA
NAOMI
NARALA
NARCELLE
NARISSA
NARLENE
NASIA
NATA
NATALIE
NATARA
NATASHA

NATION
NATIRA
NATTIE
NAVY
NAYA
NAYAN
NEA
NEALEY
NEALY
NEBA
NEDA
NEDRA
NEEELEY
NEENAH
NEINA
NELCH
NELDA
NELIA
NELL
NELLIE
NELLIENE
NELLINA
NELMA
NELVINA
NEMY
NERA
NERISSA
NESEY
NESSA
NETA
NETTA
NEVA
NEVADA
NEVE
NEVELYN
NIA
NIANI

NICA
NICHOLS
NICOL
NICOLE
NICOLETTE
NICOLIE
NICOYA
NIECY
NIEMI
NIESHA
NIEVES
NIKA
NILANA
NILES
NILSA
NINON
NIOBE
NIRA
NITA
NIVAEH
NIVEA
NIXI
NOA
NOAMI
NOANI
NOBELS
NOBLE
NOEL
NOELLE
NOLA
NOLINA
NOLITA
NONA
NONI
NORA
NOREEN
NORENA

NOREY
NORI
NORNA
NORRIA
NOVALEE
NOVELLA
NOVENA
NOVIA
NOX
NUEVA
NUMA
NUNA
NUNIA
NURA
NURIA
NUVIA
NYASIA
NYDIA
NYLA
NYLEE
NYRA
NYSA
NYX

O

OAK
OAKES
OAKLAM
OAKLAN
OAKLEY
OANNA
OCEAN
OCEANA
OCTAVIA
ODA
ODALIS
ODE
ODELIA
ODELL
ODELLA
ODERA
ODESSA
ODILIA
OFIREA
OHANNAH
OHARA
OKO
OKSANA
OLA
OLEAH
OLEANDER
OLEIA
OLENA
OLENE
OLESIA
OLETA
OLETHA
OLIANDER

OLINDA
OLISA
OLIVE
OLIVIA
OLSEN
OLSYN
OLVERY
OLWEYN
OLYMPIA
OLYNDA
OMANA
OMANAN
OMANI
OMARI
OMAYRA
OMEGA
OMIE
OMNEY
OMNI
OMORA
OMRI
ONDER
ONDREA
ONEIDA
ONEIDRA
ONIA
ONITA
ONORA
ONYA
ONYXX
OPAL
OPALINA
OPHELIA
OPHIRA
OPRAH
ORA
ORACIA

ORACLE
ORALIE
ORCHARD
ORCHID
ORDAN
ORDELLA
OREA
OREGON
ORELLA
ORI
ORIANNA
ORIANNE
ORILLA
ORIN
ORIOLE
ORITA
ORLAND
ORLEAN
ORMANDA
ORNA
ORRIAL
ORTHIA
ORY
OSANA
OSEN
OSHEA
OSHENA
OSNI
OSTIA
OTHELL
OTHELLA
OTHELLO
OTILLIA
OTTALYN
OVANNA
OVEDA
OWENA

OZARA
OZELINA
OZORA
OZORNA
OZRA
OZRI
OZZYLYN

P

PADDEN
PADDYN
PADEN
PAGEN
PAIGE
PAIGES
PAINTE
PAISLEY
PAISON
PAIVA
PALACE
PALEY
PALIN
PALLADIN
PALLAS
PALM
PALMA
PALMAR
PALMES
PALOMA
PALONA
PALYN
PANDORA
PAOLA
PARIS
PARISH
PARLEY
PARNES
PARREN
PARROTT
PARYTH
PATRICE
PATRINA

PATTISON
PAYAN
PAYCE
PAYLON
PAYSYN
PAYTON
PEACE
PEACHES
PEAKE
PEAR
PEARL
PEARLA
PEARLIE
PELIN
PELON
PENDANT
PENDER
PENELOPE
PENLEY
PEONY
PEPIN
PEPPER
PERAL
PERCIVAL
PERLANCE
PERRI
PERRIS
PERRYN
PERSIA
PERSIAN
PERSIS
PETRUS
PETUNIA
PEYTON
PFEIFFER
PHAEDRA
PHALIN

PHARIS
PHARRINGTON
PHEBA
PHEDRA
PHILA
PHILAINA
PHILANA
PHILANDER
PHILANDRIS
PHILAYNA
PHILEMON
PHILENA
PHILLIE
PHIONA
PHLEGEN
PHOEBE
PHOENIX
PHYLLIS
PIERS
PILAR
PINK
PINKSTON
PIPER
PITA
PIXIE
PLACID
PLANCYN
PLATINUM
PLUM
POET
POETRY
POLINA
POLLY
POLLYANNA
PONDER
PONDERS
POPPY

PORA
PORSHA
PORTIA
POSH
POWDER
PRAIR
PRAIRE
PRAIRIE
PRAIRIES
PRASANNA
PRAYER
PRAYERS
PRECIOUS
PRENTICE
PRESLEY
PRICILLIA
PRIESTLEY
PRINCESS
PRINCILLA
PRISSY
PRISTINA
PRITTI
PROMISE
PROPHET
PROSPEN
PROSPER
PROSPERITY
PROVENCE
PROVIDENCE
PRUDENCE
PRYANNA
PRYER
PURITY
PYERA
PYRENA
PYRIA
PYTHIA

Q

QUANAH
QUANDA
QUANTELLA
QUANTINA
QUARREN
QUEEN
QUEENA
QUENBY
QUESLIN
QUESTLIN
QUESTLINE
QUETA
QUIANA
QUILLE
QUINCYLLE
QUINELLA
QUINOA
QUINTA
QUIRIN
QUSSIA
QUYINE
QUINISE

R

RACHE
RACHEL
RACHELLE
RACHEN
RACHENE
RACINDA
RACYN
RADA
RADINA
RADLEY
RAE
RAENN
RAIDA
RAIDEN
RAILE
RAILEE
RAIN
RAINE
RAINER
RAINES
RAINEY
RALENDA
RALEY
RALIEGH
RALISSA
RALYN
RALYNE
RAMENA
RAMONA
RAMSAY
RAMSEY
RANCYE
RANDA

RANDEN
RANDI
RANDYLL
RANIELLE
RANSLEY
RANSOM
RAPTURE
RAQUEL
RAQUELLI
RAVADA
RAVI
RAVIN
RAYDA
RAYLENDA
RAYNA
RAYONA
RAYSEL
REA
REACE
REAHANNA
REANNA
REASON
REBA
REBECCA
REECE
REEGAN
REEM
REES
REESE
REEVES
REGAN
REGEN
REGENT
REGINA
REIGN
REIN
REINDER

REINDERS
REINE
REINES
REISLING
REITH
RELIA
REMAH
REMEL
REMIE
REMING
REMLE
REMLEY
RENA
RENAE
RENAIR
RENDER
RENITA
RENNON
RENYLL
REVA
REVADA
REY
REYNA
REYNOLDS
RHAGAE
RHAPSODY
RHEA
RHENE
RHETA
RHIALIE
RHIANNA
RHNEA
RHODA
RHODES
RHODORA
RHOGEAN
RHONA

RHONDIE	RISLEY	RONETTE
RHONETT	RISSA	RONEY
RHONNIE	RITSA	RONI
RHONWEN	RITZ	RONNEAL
RHYANNA	RIVA	RONNI
RHYMA	RIVER	RORI
RHYME	RIVERS	ROSA
RHYMES	RIVETS	ROSAIRE
RHYS	RIYA	ROSALIA
RIA	RIZA	ROSALIE
RIALTA	RIZLYN	ROSALIND
RIANDA	RIZZO	ROSALINDE
RIANE	ROANA	ROSANNA
RIANNAH	ROANE	ROSE
RIANNON	ROANNA	ROSELLEN
RICHELLE	ROBIN	ROSENA
RICKI	ROBY	ROSETTA
RIDGELEY	ROCHELLE	ROSHELLE
RIDGES	ROCKEELA	ROSS
RIDLEY	RODA	ROWAN
RIEGAL	ROELINA	ROWENA
RIHANA	ROGEN	ROWLEY
RIKKEN	ROHANA	ROXANNA
RILAN	ROLANDA	ROXANNE
RILENA	ROLLA	ROXY
RILEY	ROLLINS	ROYAL
RIMA	ROLYN	ROZANNE
RIMME	ROMA	ROZEN
RIMMON	ROMEY	ROZINA
RIMONA	ROMILLA	RUBINA
RINA	ROMINA	RUBY
RINDA	ROMONA	RUE
RIONA	ROMY	RUFINA
RIORDAN	RONA	RULE
RIPLEY	RONDI	RULEN
RISE	RONEA	RUMAH
RISEN	RONEE	RUMER

RUMOR
RUNNER
RURI
RUSH
RUSTICE
RUSTY
RUSTYN
RUTH
RUTHIA
RUTHIE
RYANNA
RYBA
RYELL
RYELLA
RYENLINE
RYKEN
RYLEE
RYN
RYNDEN
RYNDOM
RYNE
RYNIE
RYNN
RYNNEA
RYSTAN
RYVERS

S

SABLE
SABRINA
SACHA
SADIE
SAGA
SAGAN
SAGE
SAHARA
SAIDA
SAILER
SAJEN
SALEM
SALEN
SALESTE
SALIA
SALINA
SALLIE
SALLY
SALM
SALMA
SALMONE
SALOME
SAM
SAMANTHA
SAMARA
SAMARIA
SANDERS
SANDI
SANDLIN
SANDRA
SANDREA
SANDRIA
SANDS

SANGER
SANGRIA
SANITA
SANNA
SARAFINA
SARAID
SAREE
SARAH
SARI
SARIAH
SARINA
SAROLYN
SARRIA
SASHA
SASHAY
SASSY
SATCHEL
SATCHET
SATIN
SAULTER
SAUNDERS
SAURI
SAVAGE
SAVANNAH
SAVEEN
SAVINA
SAVINE
SAVIOR
SAVONE
SAWYER
SAXON
SAXTON
SAY
SAYANA
SAYDE
SAYDEY
SAYER

SAYLEE
SAYLEM
SAYLEY
SCANT
SCANTE
SCARLETT
SCHAE
SCHAFFER
SCHEREE
SCHUYLER
SCOUT
SCYLER
SCYLLA
SEAL
SEALE
SEALEY
SEASON
SEASONS
SEATEN
SEDONA
SEEGER
SEELEY
SEIRE
SELA
SELBY
SELDA
SELENA
SELENE
SELINA
SELLARS
SELLERS
SELTHA
SEMIRA
SEMONE
SENAY
SENECA
SENGA

SENNETT	SHANILLE	SHINA
SENORA	SHANNING	SHINE
SEQUOIA	SHANOAH	SHIREE
SERAFINA	SHANTEL	SHIVER
SEREN	SHARAE	SHULA
SERENA	SHARAN	SHUNDA
SERENDITY	SHAREL	SHUNDRA
SERENITY	SHARLA	SHYNE
SEVEN	SHARLIE	SIAM
SEVERINE	SHARLYN	SIAN
SEVILLE	SHARRAN	SIBLEY
SHADA	SHASTA	SIBYE
SHADE	SHASTEEL	SIBYL
SHADOW	SHASTELLE	SID
SHAELENE	SHAWNA	SIDNEY
SHAENNA	SHAWNEE	SIDONIA
SHAHARA	SHAYLYN	SIDONY
SHAILA	SHAYNE	SIENNA
SHAINA	SHEA	SIERRA
SHAINE	SHEBA	SIGNE
SHAINEL	SHEEN	SIGOURNEY
SHAINIE	SHEFFIELD	SILENCE
SHAKIRA	SHELBA	SILINE
SHALANE	SHELBY	SILVAINE
SHALE	SHELISE	SILVANNA
SHALEE	SHELL	SILVER
SHALEY	SHELSYE	SIMONA
SHALIEGH	SHELYSE	SIMONE
SHALLEN	SHENAE	SINCLAIRE
SHALYSE	SHEPHARD	SINEAD
SHAMRA	SHERADON	SINGER
SHAN	SHERESE	SIRAH
SHANAE	SHERIN	SIRAN
SHANDEE	SHERITAN	SIRENA
SHANDIA	SHERRATON	SIRI
SHANE	SHILOH	SISLEY
SHANELLE	SHIMONE	SISSY

SISTENE	SOMERSET	STARTLEY
SISTINE	SOMMER	STASIA
SIV	SONAY	STEIN
SIVAN	SONNETT	STELLA
SIVVON	SONNIE	STELLEN
SIXX	SONOMA	STEPH
SIYONA	SONORA	STEPHANIE
SKALLA	SONOVA	STEPHI
SKYANNE	SOPHIA	STERLA
SKYE	SORAYA	STERRY
SKYLA	SOREL	STEVIE
SKYLER	SOREN	STEILLES
SLANE	SOSIE	STINSON
SLANEY	SOUTER	STIRLING
SLOAN	SPARROW	STOREY
SLOANE	SPELLAR	STORM
SLONIE	SPELLARS	STORME
SMERA	SPELLE	STORMY
SMIRNA	SPELLERS	STRADDYN
SMYRNA	SPERRY	STYLES
SNOW	SPIRIT	SUGAR
SNOWEY	SPRAGUE	SULAN
SNYDER	SPRING	SULLEY
SOFIE	SPRUCE	SULLIVAN
SOFINA	SPURLIN	SUMMER
SOFYA	STACEY	SUMMERELLEN
SOLADA	STACIA	SUMMITT
SOLANA	STARKE	SUMTER
SOLANGE	STARLENE	SUNA
SOLEIL	STARTLET	SUNDAY
SOLI	STARLIN	SUNDER
SOLIDA	STARLING	SUNER
SOLINE	STARLITE	SUNNY
SOLITA	STARLYN	SUNSHINE
SOLON	STARNE	SURENE
SOMERLY	STARNES	SURI
SOMERS	STARR	SURIA

SURINA
SUSSETTE
SWAN
SWARNA
SWAY
SUANTA
SYBIL
SYNDEY
SYENE
SYLVAN
SYLVANA
SYLVIE
SYLWIA
SYMIRA
SYMONE
SYMPHONY
SYNDAL
SYNDE
SYNETHA
SYNORA
SYRETA
SYRI

T

TABBATH
TABBY
TABEL
TABIA
TABRINA
TACEN
TACEY
TACHA
TACIE
TAELYN
TAFFY
TAGEN
TAHNA
TAI
TAIDEN
TAIGON
TAIRRA
TAITLYN
TAKENYA
TALANA
TALASSI
TALEAH
TALENT
TALI
TALIA
TALIERA
TALISE
TALULAH
TAMARA
TAMBER
TAMBRA
TAMRA
TAMRIN

TAMYA
TAMYRA
TAMYREN
TANARY
TANDI
TANDRA
TANEAL
TANGI
TANISE
TARA
TARALEE
TARALYNN
TARENA
TARIN
TARISSE
TARMY
TARVEY
TARYN
TASMINA
TASMIND
TATUM
TAVIA
TAWANA
TAWNNA
TAWNEY
TAYDEN
TAYEN
TAYLINN
TAYLON
TAYLOR
TAZMIN
TAZMIND
TEAGAN
TEAGUE
TEAGUES
TEAH
TEAK

TEALE
TEANNIE
TEARA
TEARDRA
TEARES
TELAINA
TELLER
TELSA
TEMPEST
TEMPLE
TEMPY
TENAE
TENAYA
TENDELL
TENIAH
TENLEY
TERAH
TERENA
TERESE
TERRA
TERRAH
TERRAN
TERRE
TERRENA
TERRYN
TESS
TESSA
TESSIE
THANDI
THEAYLYN
THEODOSIA
THEONE
THEORA
THERESE
THORA
THORN
THORNE

THRATCHER	TORNETTE	TRY
TIA	TORRANCE	TRYNA
TIAMA	TORRENCE	TUESDAY
TIAN	TORRENT	TULSA
TIANA	TORRIN	TUSTI
TIARA	TORSH	TWAIN
TIBBIE	TOURAN	TWILA
TIBBY	TOVA	TWYANA
TIENA	TRACE	TYCE
TIERAH	TRACYN	TYE
TIERAN	TRAINA	TYLA
TIERNA	TRAINER	TYLERA
TIFFANY	TRANCE	TYNDALL
TIFFIN	TRAVA	TYNDEL
TIFIN	TRAYSHA	TYRA
TILANA	TRELLA	TYRINA
TILDA	TREND	
TILIRA	TRERISE	
TINDER	TRESCA	
TINDSLEY	TRESS	
TIONNE	TRESSA	
TIRA	TRESSIE	
TISA	TRICIA	
TISH	TRILBY	
TOBIA	TRINA	
TOLSON	TRINDA	
TOLSYN	TRINITY	
TONAYA	TRISHELLE	
TONEY	TRISTA	
TONYA	TRISTE	
TOPANGA	TRISTEN	
TOPAZ	TRIXIE	
TORA	TRORRY	
TORALYNN	TROUP	
TOREN	TRUDY	
TORI	TRULY	
TORNAI	TRUU	

U

UDELLA
UELA
UGANDA
ULANDA
ULANI
ULATHA
ULINA
ULLA
ULYSSIA
UMA
UMBRIA
UMBRIELLA
UNA
UNDRA
UNICE
UNIQUE
UNITY
URIA
URICE
URSA
URSULA
URVINE
URY
USHER
UTICA

V

VADA
VAISA
VAL
VALA
VALE
VALECIA
VALENA
VALENCIA
VALERA
VALERIE
VALETA
VALISTA
VALLEA
VALLEN
VALLEY
VALLORIE
VALYN
VALYNDA
VANAY
VANDA
VANEEN
VANESSA
VANI
VANITY
VANNA
VANORA
VANTHE
VARA
VARIN
VARINA
VARNA
VASHI
VASIN

VEADA
VEDA
VEGA
VEGAS
VEIL
VEILAND
VEL
VELAND
VELINDA
VELLE
VELVET
VELYNE
VEMBER
VENDA
VENETA
VENETIA
VENETTA
VENEY
VENICE
VENIS
VENITIA
VEOLA
VERA
VERAINA
VERAINE
VERDA
VERDE
VERDELLE
VERDETTLE
VERE
VERINA
VERITY
VERLYN
VERVE
VESTA
VESTER
VETA

VEVINA
VI
VIANA
VIANCA
VIANNA
VICTORIA
VIDA
VIDELLA
VIENNA
VIERA
VIERRA
VILDA
VILLARD
VILLORIA
VIMALA
VINA
VINE
VINELLE
VINES
VINTAGE
VINYARD
VIOLA
VIOLET
VIRGINIA
VIRTUE
VITA
VIV
VIVA
VIVI
VIVIA
VIVIAN
VIVICA
VIXAN
VIXEN
VIYETTE
VOLA
VOLETTA

VOLINA
VONDA
VONESE
VOYAGE
VULCAN
VYE
VYERA
VYONNE

W

WAITE
WALENA
WALONA
WALTZ
WANITA
WARNER
WARRANT
WATERS
WAVERLY
WAYLA
WENDY
WENETTA
WESTERN
WHATLEY
WHELEAN
WHIDDON
WHISPER
WHITLEY
WHITYLYN
WHITNEY
WHITTEN
WHITTER
WILDE
WILDES
WILES
WILLA
WILLOW
WILONA
WIND
WINDE
WINDER
WINDI
WINDREY

WINIFRED
WINNIE
WINONA
WINTER
WIREN
WISDOM
WISTERIA
WITHERS
WONDER
WOODES
WOODINE
WORD
WORSHIP
WOVEN
WOWENA
WRANDIE
WREN
WRENDI
WRISTON
WYLA
WYLD
WYLDER
WYNELL
WYNN
WYNNDI
WYNNE
WYNTER
WYNTRESS
WYOMIE
WYOMING
WYTHE

X

XANDRA
XARA
XAVINA
XENA
XENIAH
XIMARA
XYLA
XYSTE

Y

YURI
YZABEL
YZABELLA

YALENA
YALONDA
YAMILLE
YAMIN
YANA
YANNA
YARINE
YASHA
YASMINA
YASMINE
YAVONNA
YAZMIN
YELENA
YEMAYA
YERIEL
YESMIN
YESSI
YETTA
YEVA
YINA
YOANNA
YOCHANA
YOELLA
YOHANNA
YOHANNAH
YOLANDA
YORDAN
YORI
YOUNGER
YOVAN
YSABEL
YSABELLA
YULAN

Z

ZABRINA
ZADA
ZADIE
ZAHIRA
ZAIA
ZAIDA
ZAILYNN
ZAINA
ZAIRA
ZAIRE
ZAKIYAH
ZALE
ZALES
ZAMILLA
ZANA
ZANDRA
ZANDREA
ZANDY
ZANI
ZANIAH
ZARA
ZARAIH
ZARIAH
ZARIN
ZARINA
ZAYA
ZAYNA
ZAYRA
ZEANE
ZELAH
ZELDIA
ZELIA
ZELINA

ZELL
ZELLA
ZELMA
ZELNORA
ZELVERAI
ZENA
ZESTA
ZETA
ZEVERAE
ZHANE
ZHANNA
ZHEN
ZHENIA
ZILA
ZIMA
ZIMRAN
ZINA
ZINN
ZINNIA
ZIONA
ZIVA
ZOE
ZOELLA
ZOHARA
ZOLA
ZOLEE
ZOLEY
ZONICE
ZORA
ZORINA
ZORNA
ZOWIE
ZUDORA
ZULAH
ZUREN
ZURI
ZYAN

ZYREA
ZYREE

BOYS

A

AABID
AARIC
AARON
ABACUS
ABBOTT
ABDUL
ABE
ABEL
ABNER
ABRAHAM
ABRAM
ABRIL
ACE
ACHARD
ACKER
ACKERLEY
ACREE
ACTON
ADAIR
ADAM
ADAN
ADAR
ADDAE
ADDIS
ADDISON
ADEL
ADEN
ADIGAN
ADKIN
ADLAY
ADLER
ADNEE
ADOM

ADRIAN
ADYN
AEDAN
AEGLE
AERIN
AERON
AESON
AFAN
AGAN
AGNAR
AGNER
AGRON
AHAB
AHMOS
AIDEN
AIERY
AIGER
AIKEN
AIKER
AIME
AINSLEY
AJAX
AJAY
AKE
AKIL
AKILLES
AKINS
AKREN
AKSEL
ALANDER
ALASTAIR
ALBANY
ALBE
ALBIE
ALCOTT
ALDEE
ALDEN

ALDER
ALDEST
ALDO
ALDRED
ALDRICH
ALDRIN
ALDWYN
ALDYN
ALEC
ALECS
ALEK
ALENE
ALEX
ALEXANDIA
ALFORD
ALLARD
ALLERTON
ALLINGTON
ALLISTER
ALLWARD
ALLWEN
ALPIN
ALPS
ALTA
ALTHERTON
ALTON
ALVAN
ALVORD
AMAN
AMAURA
AMBLIN
AMBREL
AMEL
AMERICA
AMES
AMIN
AMIT

AMMON	ARCEN	ASPEN
AMON	ARCH	ASTIN
AMORY	ARCHARD	ASTON
AMOS	ARCHER	ASTOR
AMRAN	ARCHIBALD	ASWIN
ANANA	ARCHIE	ATAM
ANCEL	ARDAN	ATHAN
ANCHOR	ARDEE	ATKIN
ANDERSON	ARIAN	ATKINS
ANDRE	ARKEN	ATLAS
ANDREN	ARLAND	ATLEY
ANDRETTI	ARLE	ATOM
ANDREW	ARLEN	ATON
ANDY	ARLEY	ATTICUS
ANGEL	ARMAN	ATWATER
ANGLE	ARMEL	ATWELL
ANGLIN	ARMOND	ATWOOD
ANIL	ARNELL	ATWORTH
ANNDO	ARNIE	AUBIN
ANNISTON	ARPER	AUBREY
ANS	ARSON	AUBURN
ANSCOM	ARTIN	AUDEN
ANSEL	ARVEL	AUDIE
ANSOM	ARWEN	AUDLEY
ANSON	ARWIN	AUDREN
ANTON	ASCOT	AUGIE
ANTROY	ASH	AULTMAN
ANWEN	ASHER	AUREK
ANWYL	ASHES	AUSBURN
ANYON	ASHFORD	AUSHBURN
APEN	ASHLAND	AUSTIN
APLIN	ASHMOND	AUTHER
ARABY	ASHMOORE	AUTRY
ARBEL	ASHTON	AVDIS
ARBER	ASKEW	AVEN
ARBOR	ASLAN	AVENT
ARBOUR	ASNER	AVERY

AVNER
AVRAM
AVRAN
AVREN
AVRUM
AXE
AXIL
AXTON
AYDEN
AYDIN
AYERS
AYLEN
AYLWARD
AYMAN
AYSON
AZAR
AZIM
AZMON
AZMOND
AZRAE
AZZIE

B

BACH
BACON
BAER
BAGLEY
BAIER
BAILEY
BAILOR
BAINES
BAIRD
BAKER
BALAN
BALDER
BALDRIDGE
BALDWIN
BALLARD
BALSAM
BANCROFT
BAND
BANDER
BANDERS
BANDIT
BANDY
BANE
BANJO
BANKS
BANKSTON
BANNING
BAPTIST
BAR
BARCLAY
BARDEM
BARDEN
BAREND

BARICK
BARING
BARISON
BARK
BARKER
BARLEY
BARMAN
BARN
BARNER
BARNES
BARNETTE
BARNUM
BARRAGON
BARRETT
BARRINGTON
BARRON
BARTH
BARWICK
BASFORD
BASS
BASSETT
BASTIEN
BASWELL
BATCH
BATES
BAXTER
BAYARD
BAYDEN
BAYDON
BAYES
BAYLOR
BAYS
BAYSE
BEACAN
BEACH
BEACHER
BEACON

BEAGAN
BEALE
BEAMON
BEAN
BEATE
BEATY
BEAUCHAMP
BECK
BECKER
BECKETT
BEESON
BELDING
BELDON
BELLAMY
BELLMAN
BELTON
BENCE
BENDER
BENES
BENN
BENNEY
BENNING
BENNINGTON
BENSEY
BENSON
BENTLEY
BENTON
BERG
BERGEN
BERGER
BERIT
BERKE
BERKLEY
BERKS
BERMAN
BERTRAM
BERTRAN

BERTREN	BLENDAN	BOVEY
BERWYN	BLOCK	BOWDEN
BERYL	BLOCKER	BOWEN
BEVAN	BLOWDEN	BOWIE
BEVIL	BOAT	BOWLING
BEXLEY	BOATEN	BOWMAN
BICE	BOATWYN	BOWNAN
BICKEN	BOAZ	BOYCE
BICKLEY	BOBBYRAY	BOYD
BILSON	BODEN	BOYER
BINDEN	BODHI	BOYNTON
BINGHAM	BODI	BRACK
BIRCH	BODINE	BRACKER
BIRCHARD	BOGAN	BRACKSON
BIRD	BOISE	BRADEN
BIRGER	BOLAN	BRADFORD
BIRKETT	BOLDER	BRADLEE
BIRKEY	BOLTON	BRADSHAW
BIRLEY	BOMBER	BRAY
BISHOP	BOND	BRAGEN
BIVEN	BONGO	BRAGG
BLACKWELL	BONNER	BRAGGS
BLADE	BONYER	BRAISON
BLAINE	BOOKER	BRAIT
BLAINEN	BOONE	BRAITH
BLAISE	BOOTH	BRAITHEN
BLAKELY	BOOTS	BRALEE
BLAME	BORDEN	BRAM
BLANDON	BORDER	BRAMBLE
BLANDFORD	BOSCOE	BRAMLETT
BLANTON	BOSLEY	BRAN
BLAYNEY	BOSTON	BRANAGE
BLAYNN	BOSWELL	BRANCH
BLAZE	BOULDIN	BRANDT
BLAZER	BOURBAN	BRANIGAN
BLEN	BOUREY	BRANNON
BLEND	BOURNE	BRANSON

BRANT
BRANTEN
BRANWELL
BRANWEN
BRASON
BRAWLEY
BRAX
BRAXLEN
BRAXTEN
BRAY
BRAYLEN
BRAYLON
BRECKIN
BREEDAN
BRELAND
BRENDAN
BRENNAN
BRENTH
BRENTLEY
BRETT
BRETTON
BREWSTER
BRIANT
BRIAR
BRIARS
BRICE
BRICKER
BRIDGE
BRIDGES
BRIERS
BRIG
BRIGGS
BRIGHAM
BRILEY
BRINK
BRINKS
BRINSON

BRISTAN
BRISTOL
BRITT
BRIXON
BRIXSON
BROCK
BROCKSTON
BROCKTON
BRODER
BRODIN
BRODNEY
BRODY
BROGAN
BROGHAN
BROM
BROMLEY
BRON
BRONSON
BRONWYN
BROOKER
BROOKERD
BROOKINGS
BROOKS
BROSNAN
BROWN
BROWNING
BROWYN
BROZE
BRUCK
BRUCKER
BRUIN
BRYAND
BRYANTT
BRYCEN
BRYDEN
BRYDSON
BRYER

BRYERS
BRYSON
BRYTHE
BRYTON
BUCHANNON
BUCK
BUCKLEY
BUCKSTON
BUELE
BULLARD
BULLOCK
BURCH
BURCHERD
BURDETTE
BURDINE
BURGESS
BURKES
BURLEIGH
BURNE
BURNELL
BURNES
BURNHAM
BURNS
BURRELL

C

CAB
CABE
CABLE
CABOT
CADBURY
CADDOCK
CADE
CADEN
CADMAN
CAELAN
CAGE
CAI
CAICE
CAIDEN
CAIN
CAINE
CAJE
CALAIS
CALDEN
CALDER
CALE
CALEB
CALLAHAN
CALLSTER
CALLOWAY
CALLUM
CALON
CAM
CAMDEN
CAMEN
CAMON
CAMP
CAMPBELL

CAMPEN
CAMPION
CANAAN
CANDER
CANNON
CANTON
CANYON
CAP
CAPTAIN
CARAWAY
CARBRY
CARDEN
CARLIN
CARISLE
CARLOW
CARLSEN
CARLSON
CARTON
CARNELL
CARNES
CARP
CARPER
CARR
CARRINGTON
CARRS
CARSLEY
CARSON
CARSWELL
CARTER
CARTWRIGHT
CARVER
CASDEN
CASH
CASHLEY
CASON
CASPER
CASPIAN

CASSIDY
CASWELL
CATCHE
CATON
CAULDER
CAULDREN
CAVEN
CAYDEN
CAYE
CEABRON
CEASE
CECIL
CEDAR
CELSO
CELUM
CELVAN
CENDER
CERF
CERVANT
CESAR
CHABE
CHADEN
CHADLEY
CHADWICK
CHAINES
CHAINEY
CHAKER
CHALEN
CHALLEN
CHALMER
CHALON
CHAMBERS
CHAN
CHANCE
CHAND
CHANDER
CHANDLEY

CHANEY
CHANNER
CHANNING
CHANON
CHANS
CHAPEN
CHAPLIN
CHAPMAN
CHARLEY
CHARLTON
CHAS
CHASE
CHASON
CHAT
CHATWIN
CHAUNCEY
CHAY
CHAZ
CHAZON
CHENEY
CHENSON
CHEST
CHESTER
CHESTON
CHET
CHETNY
CHETWIN
CHEVEN
CHEVER
CHEVY
CHILTON
CHIN
CHIP
CHIPPER
CHORDE
CHORDEN
CHRISLER

CHRISTIAN
CHURCHE
CHUX
CID
CIGLER
CINCO
CIRRUS
CISCO
CISTO
CIVILLE
CLANCE
CLANCY
CLANEY
CLANTON
CLARK
CLARKSON
CLAVEN
CLAVEY
CLAWDELL
CLAYWELL
CLEARY
CLEG
CLEM
CLEMENT
CLEVE
CLIFF
CLIFTON
CLINE
CLIPPER
CLIVE
CLOONEY
CLOYD
CLUE
COACH
COASTAL
COBE
CODE

CODY
COE
COHEN
COLBAN
COLBY
COLBYN
COLDEN
COLDIN
COLE
COLEBAN
COLEMAN
COLEN
COLERIDGE
COLEY
COLGAN
COLLEY
COLLIER
COLLIN
COLLINS
COLLIS
COLSTEN
COLSTER
COLT
COLTER
COLY
COLYN
COMBS
CONAIR
CONGER
CONLAND
CONNAWAY
CONNELL
CONNERY
CONNIE
CONRAN
CONROY
CONWAY

CONWELL
CONYER
COOKE
COOKES
COOLING
COOPER
COPPER
CORBIN
CORBY
CORBYN
CORDEN
COREY
CORGAN
CORIANDER
CORLIN
CORMAC
CORNEY
CORONA
CORTLAND
CORVAN
CORWYN
COTHRAN
COTTER
COTTON
COULTER
COUNT
COUNTRY
COURT
COURTNEY
COVE
COX
COY
CRAFT
CRAINE
CRANDEL
CRANSTON
CRAVEY

CRAWFORD
CRAWLE
CRAWLEY
CRAYTON
CREASON
CREED
CREEDANCE
CREEK
CREEKES
CREEKSON
CREIGHTON
CRENSHAW
CRESP
CREST
CRET
CREWES
CREWS
CRICHTON
CRILER
CRISPIN
CRITON
CRITTON
CROCKER
CROCKETT
CROFT
CROFTON
CROMER
CROSBY
CROSTON
CROTHERS
CROWLE
CROWLEY
CROWSON
CRUE
CRUZ
CRYLER
CULKIN

CULLEN
CULLEY
CURB
CURBEY
CURRY
CURUTHERS
CUSTER
CUTLER
CUTTES
CUTTS
CUYLER
CYBOR
CYDER
CYE
CYGAN

D

DABNEY
DABRIEL
DABRY
DADE
DAGEN
DAGGER
DAGWOOD
DAHL
DAK
DAKEN
DAKOTA
DALANEY
DALLAS
DALLEY
DALT
DALTON
DAMEN
DAMIEN
DAMON
DAMONE
DAND
DANE
DANEY
DANIR
DANLE
DANNER
DANSFORD
DANTON
DARBRY
DARBY
DARCY
DARMAN
DARNELL

DARREN
DARRIS
DARSEY
DARTON
DARVY
DASH
DASHER
DASON
DATHAN
DAUGHTRY
DAVIE
DAVIES
DAVIN
DAVIS
DAVY
DAWBER
DAWK
DAWKINS
DAWSON
DAX
DAXON
DAXTER
DAXTON
DAYER
DAYLEN
DAYSON
DAYTEN
DAYTON
DEABLO
DEACON
DEAL
DEAN
DEANS
DECK
DECKER
DECLARE
DEETER

DEGAN
DEHL
DEIGAN
DEKE
DELANEY
DELBRIDGE
DELE
DELMORE
DELPHIN
DELT
DELTON
DEMMING
DEMP
DEMPS
DEMPSEY
DENDBY
DENDY
DENHAM
DENIM
DENK
DENLEY
DENMAN
DENNARD
DENNIE
DENNON
DENT
DENTON
DENZEL
DENZIE
DEP
DERBY
DERIAN
DERISO
DERLAM
DERLIN
DERRY
DERYN

DESLEY	DIRK	DOON
DESMOND	DIRKES	DORAL
DESTER	DISICK	DORAN
DESTIN	DISON	DORE
DETRY	DIX	DOREY
DETTON	DIXON	DORGAN
DEUCE	DIZON	DORIAN
DEUTER	DOAN	DORMAN
DEVER	DOBBIN	DORN
DEVEREU	DOBBINS	DORSET
DEVEROE	DOBBS	DORSEY
DEVERON	DOBBYN	DOTHAN
DEVIN	DOBIE	DOVER
DEWARD	DOBINE	DOWELL
DEWAY	DOBRY	DOWEN
DEWEY	DOCK	DOX
DEWI	DOCKER	DOYAL
DEWITT	DOCKES	DOYLE
DEX	DODD	DOZIER
DEZ	DODGE	DRACEY
DEZI	DODSON	DRACHEN
DHANI	DOHERTY	DRAEGAN
DHILLON	DOLCE	DRAELYN
DIAMONTE	DOGAN	DRAKE
DIANTE	DOLLESTER	DRAKER
DICKENS	DOLLIS	DRALYN
DICKSON	DOLON	DRAPER
DIESEL	DOLPH	DRAVEN
DIGBY	DOLSON	DRAY
DIGG	DOM	DRAYLEN
DIGGER	DOMERO	DREDEN
DILL	DOMINIC	DRENNAN
DILLAN	DONLEY	DREY
DILSON	DONNAN	DRIDGE
DINS	DONNELL	DRIVER
DINSDALE	DONOVAN	DROVER
DINSMORE	DOOLEY	DRUER

DRUM

DRUMMOND

DRURY

DRYDEN

DRYSON

DRYSTAN

DUBLIN

DUCK

DUDE

DUDLEY

DUFF

DUFFIELD

DUFFY

DUGAN

DUNBAR

DUNCAN

DUNDEE

DUNHAM

DUNK

DUNN

DUNNING

DUNSTON

DUNT

DUPRE

DUPREE

DURHAM

DURKE

DURRAN

DURRE

DURWIN

DUSK

DUSKIN

DUSKY

DUSTER

DUSTIN

DUSTY

DUTCH

DUTTON

DUVAN

DWIGHTON

DWYER

DWYKE

DYLE

DYM

DYRE

DYRON

DYSE

E

EAGAN
EAMES
EAMON
EAN
EARL
EARLEN
EARLY
EARON
EARVIN
EASON
EAST
EASTBUR
EASTERN
EASTON
EATON
EBAL
EBAN
EBEN
EBREL
EBON
ECHARD
ECKERS
ECKERSON
ECKLEE
ECKLEY
ECTOR
EDAN
EDDYSON
EDEL
EDEN
EDENSON
EDGE
EDGES
EDISON

EDON
EDRICK
EDSON
EDSYN
EDWARD
EDWARDS
EDWIGES
EDWIN
EDWYN
EFRON
EFTON
EGAN
EGBORN
EGER
EGERTON
EGLE
EGMON
EGON
EIDSON
EIRES
EITAN
EITON
EIVE
EKELS
ELAN
ELDEN
ELDER
ELDRIDGE
ELEX
ELGER
ELGIN
ELHAM
ELI
ELIAS
ELIASON
ELIC
ELIJAH

ELICK
ELKAN
ELKE
ELKELS
ELLER
ELLERTON
ELLINGTON
ELLION
ELLIOT
ELLIS
ELLSWORTH
ELMAN
ELMOT
ELTON
ELVEN
ELVIN
ELWEN
ELWOOD
ELY
EMENY
EMERY
EMITT
EMJAY
EMMONS
EMORY
EMRIC
ENAN
ENDER
ENGLES
ENGLAND
ENNIS
ENSOR
ENVER
EPIC
EPLEY
ERA
ERAN

ERBY
ERCHEL
ERHARDT
ERIN
ERLAND
ERRETT
ERROL
ERVE
ERVIN
ESPEN
ESPY
ESTES
ESTIN
ETAN
ETHAN
ETHREN
ETHRIDGE
ETWIN
EUAL
EUDIN
EURAL
EURBY
EVAN
EVANDER
EVANS
EVEL
EVEN
EVEREST
EVERETTE
EVERS
EVERTON
EVETT
EVRES
EVRET
EWALD
EWAN
EWEN

EWING
EXOD
EXZEL
EYTIN
EZRA
EZRON

F

FABIAN
FACEN
FACTOR
FADEN
FADON
FAGEN
FAGON
FAINE
FAIRBANKS
FAIRES
FAIRON
FALLEN
FALLEY
FALLIN
FALLON
FANNING
FANNON
FANT
FARKUS
FARLEY
FARMER
FARRELL
FARREN
FARRIS
FARROW
FARWELL
FASE
FATHOM
FAULK
FAULKNER
FAVOR
FAXON
FEARCE
FEARS

FELDER
FELISE
FELMAN
FELTON
FENDER
FENN
FENNELL
FENNER
FENWICK
FERGUS
FERGUSON
FERN
FERNE
FERNLEY
FERRAND
FERRELL
FERRIS
FERYLL
FEVEN
FIELDEN
FIELDER
FIELDING
FIELDS
FIEN
FIFER
FILMORE
FILSON
FIN
FINBARR
FINCH
FINCHER
FINDLEY
FINDOM
FINLAN
FINLEY
FINN
FINNEY

FINTAN
FINTON
FIRMAN
FISCHER
FITCH
FITZGERALD
FLAIR
FLAME
FLANDERS
FLANN
FLANNEN
FLANNERY
FLANNIGAN
FLANT
FLASS
FLAYNE
FLEET
FLEETWOOD
FLEMING
FLEMMER
FLEMMING
FLETCHER
FLINT
FLOAN
FLOURER
FLOWERS
FLYER
FLYNN
FLYNT
FOGLE
FOLAN
FOLEY
FOLKE
FOLLIS
FOLSOM
FORD
FORDAN

FORDHAM
FOREIGN
FOREMAN
FOREND
FORGE
FORREST
FORT
FORTH
FOST
FOSTER
FOWLER
FOX
FRAILE
FRAINE
FRALEY
FRALIN
FRANKIE
FRANKLIN
FRAYLEY
FRAZE
FREDDER
FREE
FREEBORN
FREED
FREELER
FREEMAN
FREMONT
FREWEN
FREY
FRIDMAN
FRIEDMAN
FRIEDER
FRITZ
FROST
FROSTEN
FRY
FRYER

FRYERS
FULKE
FULLER
FULLERTON
FULTON
FURMAN
FURY
FYE
FYNDHAM

G

GABE
GABLE
GABLIN
GABREL
GABRIEL
GABSON
GACEY
GACON
GAETAN
GAGAN
GAGE
GAEN
GAGER
GAINES
GALDIN
GALEN
GALON
GALTON
GALVIN
GALWAY
GAMVLE
GAMMON
GAMN
GANNON
GANYON
GARDEN
GARDENER
GAREK
GARETH
GARF
GARIN
GARMAN
GARMEN

GARNER
GARNET
GARON
GARREN
GARRETT
GARRISON
GARTH
GARVAN
GARVEN
GARVER
GARVEY
GARVIN
GARYLEN
GASE
GASKINS
GASON
GASTON
GATES
GATHAN
GATHEN
GATLIN
GAVEN
GAVIN
GAVIT
GAYLAND
GAYLORD
GAYNOR
GAYTON
GEER
GENDRIN
GENO
GENOAH
GENT
GENTLE
GENTREE
GENTRY
GERBEN

GERE
GERRIT
GERSH
GERWYN
GESHAM
GETHIN
GHALBY
GHASSAN
GIANN
GIBB
GIBBON
GIBBONS
GIBSON
GIDEON
GIDON
GIFFON
GIFFORD
GIG
GIGGS
GIL
GILBY
GILES
GILI
GILL
GILLANDER
GILLES
GILLEY
GILMAN
GILMORE
GILROY
GILSON
GINTON
GIVEN
GIVENS
GIVON
GLACIER
GLACIERS

GLADSTON
GLADSTONE
GLAINE
GLAISON
GLASSON
GLENARD
GLENDALE
GLENDON
GLENDYL
GLENMORE
GLENNON
GLENWARD
GOBI
GODDAR
GODFREY
GODWIN
GOGEN
GOLDEN
GONZ
GOODAN
GOODREAU
GOODRICH
GOODROW
GOONES
GOPIN
GORBAN
GORBEN
GORDY
GORE
GOREN
GOSS
GOSSLING
GOWDIN
GOWDY
GOWEN
GOWER
GRABLE

GRADDY
GRADIN
GRADY
GRAEME
GRAFTON
GRAHAM
GRAILE
GRAINE
GRAINES
GRAM
GRANGE
GRANT
GRANTLAND
GRANTLY
GRATTON
GRAVEL
GRAVES
GRAVITT
GRAYDON
GRAYER
GRAYLAN
GRAYLAND
GRAYLEY
GRAYLON
GRAYSON
GRAYTON
GREELEY
GREENWOOD
GRESHAM
GRETT
GRICE
GRIDEN
GRIDGER
GRIER
GRIFFIN
GRIFFITH
GRIGGS

GRIGSBY
GRINER
GRIP
GRISHAM
GRITT
GROVE
GROVER
GRYTON
GUARD
GUARDS
GUNION
GUNN
GUNNAR
GUNTER
GUSKE
GUSTIN
GUY
GUYON
GWENDELL
GWENT
GYDON
GYLES
GYSEN
GYSLEY

H

HABOR
HACKETT
HACKMAN
HADLEE
HADLEY
HADRAN
HADWEN
HADWIN
HAGEN
HAGGARD
HAIM
HAINES
HAL
HALDEN
HALEN
HALEND
HALL
HALLES
HALSEY
HALSTON
HALTON
HAMEL
HAMILTON
HAMLIN
HAMM
HAMMET
HAMMIE
HAMMOND
HAMON
HAMP
HAMPTON
HAND
HANDERS

HANIGAN
HANS
HANSON
HARBIN
HARBOR
HARBOUR
HARDEN
HARDIE
HARDY
HARGRAVE
HARKEN
HARLAND
HARLOW
HARMON
HARNES
HARPE
HARPER
HARRINGOTN
HARRIS
HARRISON
HARTIGAN
HARTLEY
HARTWELL
HARUM
HARVARD
HARVEY
HASKEL
HASTINGS
HATCHER
HAWKES
HAWKINS
HAWKS
HAYDEN
HAYES
HAYNES
HAYWARD
HAZARD

HAZE
HAZZARD
HEALEY
HEALY
HEARN
HEARST
HEATH
HEELEY
HEIN
HEINZ
HEISLEY
HELLER
HELLERTON
HELMAN
HELMS
HELSEY
HENDER
HENDERSON
HENDLEY
HENDRIX
HENLEY
HENRI
HENSLEY
HENSON
HENTON
HERNDON
HERRIN
HERRINGTON
HERSCHEL
HERSHALL
HESTON
HEXTON
HEYWARD
HEYWOOD
HIATT
HICKES
HICKS

HIERS	HOWE
HIGGINS	HOWLAN
HILL	HOWLAND
HILLARD	HUBER
HILLES	HUCK
HILLSMAN	HUDSON
HILTON	HUELITT
HINDER	HUEWITT
HINES	HUGH
HIRAM	HUGHE
HIRSH	HUGHES
HIXON	HUITT
HOBBES	HULAND
HOBBS	HULL
HOBSON	HULSEY
HODGE	HUME
HODGES	HUMPHREY
HOGAN	HUNTER
HOLDEN	HURLEY
HOLDER	HURST
HOLLAND	HURSTON
HOLLINS	HUSTON
HOLLIS	HUTCH
HOLMES	HUTCHINS
HOLSEY	HUTCHINSON
HOLT	HUTTON
HOLTEN	HYATT
HOLTON	HYDEN
HOLYN	HYGHNER
HOOKES	HYLAN
HOOP	HYLAND
HOOPER	HYLL
HOOVER	HYMAN
HOKINS	
HORRACE	
HOUSER	
HOUSTON	

I

IAGAN
IAIN
IAN
IATHAN
IBSON
IKE
INDIE
INDY
INGALLS
INGRAM
INMAN
IRA
IRAN
IRV
IRVE
IRVIN
IRVING
IRWIN
ISAAC
IVAN
IVERY
IVES
IVON

J

JABE
JABIN
JABON
JACE
JACEN
JACKSON
JACKSTON
JACOB
JACOBY
JAD
JADAAN
JADE
JADEN
JADRAN
JADWIN
JAGEN
JAGER
JAGGER
JAIDAN
JAKYN
JALEN
JAMESON
JAMISON
JAMON
JANSEN
JANTZEN
JAREN
JARENT
JARON
JARONS
JARRETT
JARVEY
JARVIS

JARYN
JASE
JASPER
JASTIN
JAVEN
JAVON
JAXON
JAXSON
JAXSTON
JAYE
JAYLON
JAYMES
JAZZ
JEB
JED
JEDSON
JEFFERS
JEFFERSON
JENKINS
JENNER
JENNINGS
JENNISON
JENSON
JENTRY
JEP
JERAN
JERRI
JERVEN
JESSIE
JESTIN
JETER
JETT
JEVAN
JILES
JILLIAN
JIMBO
JIMMERSON

JO
JOAQUIN
JOB
JOBIE
JOBY
JOEL
JOHAN
JOHANN
JOHNPAUL
JOHNSON
JOINER
JOLAN
JOLON
JONAS
JONATHAN
JONES
JONESEY
JONMICHAEL
JOPLIN
JORAN
JORDAN
JORGEN
JORY
JOS
JOSH
JOSS
JOSTAN
JOSTHAN
JOTHAM
JOURNEY
JOVI
JUD
JUDE
JUDGE
JUDGES
JUDSON
JULIAN

JUPE
JURGEN
JUSTE
JUSTICE
JUSTIN
JVON
JYDAN
JYDEN
JULES
JYNDON
JYREE
JYSON

K

KABE
KADE
KADEN
KADENCE
KADIAN
KAETO
KAGE
KAGEN
KAIGE
KAIL
KAIMAN
KAINE
KAIYON
KALB
KALBOT
KALE
KALEM
KALLUM
KAM
KAMDEN
KAMEN
KAMERON
KAMREN
KANDELL
KANDLE
KANNON
KANYON
KARCHER
KAREKIN
KARLIN
KARNEGY
KARNEY
KARP

KARPER
KARR
KARSON
KARST
KARTER
KASEN
KASH
KASHTON
KASON
KASS
KASTOR
KATO
KAYDE
KAYDEN
KAYIN
KAYLE
KAYLOB
KAYLOR
KAYNE
KAYSON
KAZTLER
KEANAN
KEANU
KEARNS
KEARY
KEATLEY
KEATON
KEATS
KECHEL
KEDRICK
KEELAND
KEEN
KEENAN
KEETON
KEEVIN
KEGLER
KEIFER

KEIL
KEITHAN
KELAR
KELEN
KELL
KELLEN
KELLER
KELSEY
KELSO
KELSON
KELTON
KELVIN
KEMP
KEMPER
KEMPTON
KENDALL
KENDON
KENDRELL
KENDRICK
KENNER
KENNET
KENNISON
KENSIL
KENTLEY
KENTON
KENWARD
KEPLER
KERN
KERNES
KERSEY
KERTLAND
KESTON
KETT
KETTON
KEV
KEYLAR
KHAMBRE

KHAN
KHOURI
KHYLER
KIANDRE
KIDD
KIEN
KIENE
KEIP
KIEV
KILLON
KILROY
KILSON
KIMBALL
KIMBRELL
KINCAID
KINDELL
KINDER
KINDRED
KING
KINGSTON
KINLEY
KINNEL
KIP
KIPLER
KIPLING
KIPPER
KIRKLAND
KIRKLEY
KIRKSON
KIRKWOOD
KIRVIN
KLAUSEN
KLAY
KLEEF
KLEINA
KLEM
KLEMANS

KLEMENS
KLESCO
KLINE
KLYMM
KNEEL
KNIGHT
KNIGHTON
KNOLL
KNOTEN
KNOWLES
KNOWLTON
KNOX
KNOXTON
KNUTE
KOBE
KOBI
KOBIN
KOEN
KOGAN
KOHEN
KOBLY
KOLE
KOLLEN
KOLLIER
KOLMAN
KONNER
KORBEL
KORBEN
KORBYN
KOREN
KOREY
KORIN
KORRIGAN
KORTEN
KOSNER
KOSTAS
KOSTER

KOSTNER
KOVE
KRAEL
KRAMER
KRAUSE
KRAYTON
KRESCO
KRISTIAN
KRUZ
KULLEN
KUMAR
KUNO
KUPER
KUSTER
KUTTER
KYAN
KYD
KYE
KYLAN
KYLER
KYLERTON
KYNDRED
KYNE
KYRAN
KYSON
KYSTON
KYZER

L

LABAN
LACHLAN
LACHMAN
LADDEN
LADEN
LAEL
LAFE
LAGEN
LAIRD
LAIS
LAIZER
LAKE
LAKER
LAKOTA
LAL
LAMIN
LAN
LANCE
LANCER
LANDEN
LANDER
LANDERS
LANDES
LANDFORD
LANDIS
LANDON
LANDRUM
LANDRY
LANDSON
LANDUM
LANE
LANGE
LANGDON

LANGFORD
LANGLEY
LANGSDON
LANGSTON
LANGTON
LANIER
LANNING
LANNY
LANSING
LATON
LANTZ
LANUAL
LANZO
LARAMIE
LARE
LAREDO
LARET
LARGO
LARKIN
LARNE
LARNELL
LARNES
LARON
LAROYCE
LARS
LARSE
LARSEN
LARSON
LARZ
LASHE
LASHLEY
LASKEY
LASSEN
LASSIT
LASSITER
LATHEM
LATIMER

LATTIMER
LAVAY
LAVI
LAVON
LAW
LAWSON
LAWTON
LAYLAN
LAYSY
LAYTE
LAYTON
LAZ
LAZLO
LAZO
LEAF
LEAL
LEAMON
LEAND
LEANDER
LEAR
LEARY
LEATH
LEATHER
LEAVERY
LEDYARD
LEEV
LEGEND
LEGER
LEGGETT
LEIF
LEITH
LELAND
LELDON
LELLAND
LEM
LEN
LENDON

LENDRUM	LINTON	LOTT
LENNIN	LITTON	LOTUS
LENNON	LITZ	LOUKS
LENSOR	LIVE	LOVETT
LENTON	LIVINGSTON	LOWELL
LENVIL	LLANO	LOWERY
LENZ	LLEYTON	LOYAL
LEO	LOCHAN	LUAS
LEREMY	LOCK	LUBIN
LESLIE	LOCKE	LUCA
LEVEN	LOCKES	LUCAS
LEVERETTE	LOCKRIDGE	LUDGER
LEVERTON	LODEN	LUICA
LEVI	LODGE	LUISTER
LEVIN	LODI	LUKAS
LEVY	LOFTEN	LUKE
LEW	LOGAN	LUKMAN
LEWIE	LOHAN	LUMAS
LEX	LOHDEN	LUMER
LEYDEN	LOKIE	LUNDY
LEYLAND	LOMAN	LUNT
LEYTH	LOMAS	LUSK
LIAM	LOBARD	LUTE
LIAN	LOMBARDI	LUX
LIDELL	LOMOX	LYAM
LIEGHLAND	LOND	LYDAN
LIESE	LONDON	LYE
LIESOL	LORAN	LYFE
LIMB	LORCAN	LYLE
LINC	LORD	LYMAN
LINCOLN	LORE	LYNDE
LINDELL	LOREN	LYNDELL
LINDEN	LORENS	LYNDEY
LINES	LORES	LYNDON
LINFORD	LORING	LYNE
LINK	LORNE	LYNTON
LINLEY	LOTAN	LYNWOOD

LYONS
LYRKE

M

MABRY
MAC
MACE
MACGUIRE
MACIN
MACK
MACKAY
MACKEY
MACON
MADDEN
MADDOCK
MADDOX
MADOC
MADOCK
MADON
MAGEE
MAGELLAN
MAGNUM
MAGNUS
MAHLER
MAHONEY
MAKES
MAKO
MALDEN
MALEN
MALLARD
MALLEY
MALLIN
MALONE
MALONEY
MANDER
MANDERS
MANES

MANNING
MANNIX
MANNON
MANSE
MANSON
MARCELL
MARCO
MARDELL
MARDIE
MARIS
MARKEE
MARKEY
MARKLAND
MARKS
MARKUS
MARLON
MARS
MARSDEN
MARSH
MARSHALL
MARSON
MARSTON
MARTY
MARZ
MASON
MASSEY
MATHAN
MATHERS
MATHIS
MAULDIN
MAVECK
MAVERICK
MAVIN
MAVIS
MAWAN
MAX
MAXWELL

MAYER
MAYES
MAYNARD
MAYNER
MAYOR
MAZE
MCCABE
MCCARTNEY
MCCAULEY
MCCAY
MCCLANE
MCCLURE
MCCOLLOM
MCCOOK
MCCOY
MCCRARY
MCCRAY
MCCULLEN
MCDANIEL
MCDONALD
MCFARLIN
MCGILL
MCGRAW
MCGUIRE
MCINTIRE
MCKADE
MCKAYDE
MCKELLAN
MCKINLEY
MCKINNEY
MCKOY
MCLEAN
MCMILLAN
MCNAIR
MCNEIL
MEAD
MEANT

MEARL	MITCHELL	MYREN
MEIGHS	MITCHUM	
MEL	MOBIE	
MELBOURNE	MODEIN	
MELBURN	MODI	
MELDON	MOLDEN	
MELFORD	MONROE	
MELROY	MONTFORD	
MENDEL	MONTGOMERY	
MENTON	MORELAND	
MERCER	MOREY	
MERCHANT	MORIE	
MERIT	MORIN	
MERRICK	MORLAND	
MERRILL	MORRELL	
MERRITT	MORRIS	
MERV	MORRISON	
METTS	MORRLEY	
MEYERS	MORROW	
MICHAH	MORSE	
MICK	MOSES	
MIDDLEBROOKS	MOSS	
MIKAS	MOTOR	
MIKEL	MULDER	
MILAN	MULLINS	
MILES	MURDOCK	
MILFORD	MURLIE	
MILLBANK	MURPHY	
MILLBROOK	MURRAY	
MILLER	MURRILL	
MILLS	MURT	
MINER	MYER	
MINOR	MYERS	
MINTER	MYLER	
MIRUS	MYLES	
MITCH	MYNOR	
MITCHAM	MYNTON	

N

NABIL
NABOR
NACHMAN
NACHSON
NADER
NAIN
NANDOR
NANSEN
NANSON
NAPIER
NAREN
NARRISON
NARTEN
NAS
NASA
NASH
NATE
NATH
NATHAN
NATION
NATO
NAVARRO
NAVY
NAYAN
NAYLOR
NEAF
NED
NEEKO
NEELY
NEIF
NEKANE
NELDON
NELS

NELSON
NEO
NERAL
NESBITT
NESS
NETHAN
NETS
NEVAN
NEVILLE
NEVIN
NEWBIE
NEWBURY
NEWCOMB
NEWELL
NEWLAN
NEWLAND
NEWLIN
NEWLON
NEWMAN
NEWT
NEWTON
NEYMAN
NICHOLS
NICK
NICKEL
NICKLEBY
NICKLER
NICKEY
NICO
NIELS
NIGHT
NIGHTS
NILE
NILES
NILSON
NILSSON
NIVEN

NIX
NIXON
NOAH
NOAM
NOBLE
NODEN
NODEL
NOLAN
NOLAND
NOLDEN
NOLL
NOON
NOOR
NORIN
NORRELL
NORRIS
NORRISON
NORRISTON
NORSE
NORTH
NORTON
NORWARD
NOVAE
NOWELL
NUELL
NUNRY
NYLAN
NYLAND
NYLEN
NYLES

O

OAK
OAKLAN
OAKLAND
OAKLEE
OAKLEY
OAN
OATES
OBI
OBIE
O'BRIEN
O'BRYAN
OCEAN
OCIE
O'CONNELL
ODE
ODELL
ODEM
ODEN
ODIE
ODIN
ODOLF
ODOM
O'DONNELL
OGLE
OKIE
OLAN
OLDRICH
OLIN
OLINSTEAD
OLIVER
OLLIE
OLNEY
OLSEN

OLSON
O'MALLEY
ONAN
ONDER
O'NEIL
OPIE
ORAN
ORDELL
OREGON
OREN
ORFORD
ORIAN
ORIE
ORIOL
ORISON
ORLANDO
ORLEAN
ORMOND
ORRAN
ORRENT
ORRIAL
ORRIS
ORSIN
ORSON
ORTON
ORWAY
OS
OSBORNE
OSGOOD
OSKAR
OSLO
OSMAN
OSMOND
OSRED
OSRIC
OSSIE
OSTEN

OSWALD
OSWIN
OTHMAN
OTTO
OTTOMAN
OVERTON
OVID
OWEN
OWNEY
OXE
OXFORD
OZ
OZELL
OZIEL
OZNIE
OZZIE
OZZY

P

PACE
PACER
PADDEN
PADDON
PADEN
PADGET
PADGETT
PAGE
PAGEN
PAINTE
PAISLEY
PAISON
PAKE
PALL
PALLADIN
PALLATON
PALLMEN
PALMAR
PALMER
PALTON
PANCE
PANE
PARK
PARKER
PARKES
PARKS
PARNES
PARR
PARRELL
PARREN
PARRNELL
PARROTT
PARRY

PARSON
PASCHAL
PASTOR
PATCHER
PATE
PATTERSON
PAUL
PAULIE
PALLIN
PAUN
PAVEN
PAWLEY
PAX
PAXEL
PAXTON
PAYEN
PAYLON
PAYNE
PAYSON
PAYTEX
PAZ
PEAK
PEAKE
PEALE
PEARCE
PEARLIE
PEARSON
PEAVY
PEDERSON
PEER
PEERSON
PELTON
PEMBERTON
PENDER
PENDLETON
PENLAN
PENLAND

PENLEY
PENN
PENTZ
PERCIVAL
PERCY
PERRIN
PERRY
PERRYMAN
PERSIS
PERTH
PERVIS
PETE
PEYMAN
PHARIS
PHARO
PHARPER
PHELAN
PHELGEN
PHELPS
PHENN
PHEX
PHILAN
PHILANDO
PHILEMAN
PHILLIPS
PHILMAN
PHILO
PHOENIX
PIER
PIERCE
PIERCE
PIERS
PIERSON
PIKE
PILOT
PIM
PIN

PINERO
PIPER
PIPPIN
PIRATE
PITCH
PITCHER
PITT
PITTMAN
POE
POLK
POLLARD
POLLOCK
POLO
PONDER
PONS
POOLE
POPE
PORT
PORTER
PORTLAND
POSTEN
POTTER
POUL
POWDER
POWELL
POWER
POWERS
PRAIRIE
PRATT
PRAVAT
PRAVIN
PRENTICE
PRESCOTT
PRESLEY
PREST
PRESTON
PREWITT

PRICE
PRIESTLEY
PRINCE
PRITCHARD
PROCTOR
PROP
PROPHET
PROSPEN
PROVENCE
PRUDENCE
PRUITT
PRYE
PRYOR
PUCK
PULLMAN
PULLUM
PURDY
PURLEY
PURSEY
PURVIS
PUTNAM
PYKE
PYKER
PYRE
PYRLAND

Q

QUADE
QUAID
QUAIN
QUAINT
QUAMEL
QUAN
QUANT
QUANTUM
QUARREN
QUENBY
QUENTEL
QUESTLIN
QUICK
QUIGLEY
QUINCEY
QUINLAN
QUINN
QUIRIN
QUITO
QUIX
QUON
QUSAY

R

RAB
RACE
RACEY
RACKE
RACKEL
RADFORD
RADLEY
RADNOR
RADY
RAEBURN
RAENIN
RAFE
RAFFERTY
RAIDEN
RAINER
RAKE
RAKES
RALEY
RALON
RALSTON
RALTON
RAMEL
RAMMAN
RAMP
RAMPES
RAMSAY
RAMSDEN
RAMSEY
RANCE
RANCEFORD
RANCH
RACHER
RANCYE

RAND
RANDEN
RANDIE
RANDLE
RANGE
RANGER
RANK
RANKIN
RANNON
RANON
RANSOM
RANT
RANTE
RASTEN
RASTUS
RAVEN
RAVID
RAVIN
RAVIS
RAWLE
RAWLINGS
RAWLINS
RAWSON
RAYAN
RAYBOUR
RAYCE
RAYDEN
RAYFIELD
RAYK
RAYLAND
RAYLIN
RAYNAR
RAYNARD
RAYNER
RAYON
RAYSH
RAYSON

REACE
READ
REAMAN
REANER
REARDEN
REASER
REASON
REBEL
REDD
REDFORD
REDMAN
REDMOND
REECE
REEF
REEM
REES
REESE
REESEY
REEVES
REEZ
REG
REGAL
REGANT
REID
REIDAR
REIDER
REIGN
REIN
REINDER
REINE
REINHAR
REITH
REM
REMAL
REMIAL
REMINGTON
REMLE

REMLEY	RICHTER	ROAM
REMMING	RIDDLE	ROAN
REMY	RIDGER	ROANE
RENARE	RIDGE	ROARKE
RENDER	RIDGELY	ROB
RENNELL	RIDGES	ROBESON
RENNON	RIDLEY	ROBLE
RENO	RIDVAN	ROBLES
RENSHAW	RIEGAL	ROBSON
RENSON	RIEMER	ROBY
RENTON	RIEN	ROC
RENZE	RIFLE	ROCKER
RESTE	RIGBY	ROCKETT
RESTON	RIGGENS	ROCKNEY
REV	RIGGS	ROD
REVIN	RIGSBY	RODDERICK
REWIS	RIKE	RODDY
REX	RIKER	RODEO
REY	RIKKEN	RODMAN
REYNARD	RILAN	ROEAN
REYNOLDS	RILEY	ROEL
RHAGAE	RIMME	ROGAN
RHENDON	RIMMON	ROGEN
RHETT	RINGO	ROHAN
RHODEN	RINON	ROINE
RHODES	RIP	ROLAND
RHONWEN	RIPLEY	ROLFAN
RHORIS	RISE	ROLF
RHOWEN	RITCH	ROLFIN
RHYMAN	RITT	ROLLAN
RHYS	RITTER	ROLLIE
RIANO	RIVERS	ROLLINS
RICHART	RIVERSON	ROLT
RICHER	RIVETS	ROMAN
RICHMAN	RIVINGSTON	ROMANO
RICHMON	RIZAL	ROMEO
RICHMOND	RIZO	ROMNEY

ROMO
ROMY
ROND
RONDEN
RONDI
RONEY
RONLEE
RONSON
ROOK
ROOKER
ROONEY
ROPER
RORY
ROSE
ROSK
ROSS
ROSTON
ROSWELL
ROTH
ROUD
ROVEN
ROVIN
ROWAN
ROWDEN
ROWDY
ROWE
ROWEN
ROWLEY
ROWN
ROYAL
ROYALTON
ROYCE
ROYD
ROYDEAN
ROYST
ROYSTON
RUBEN

RUCKER
RUDDER
RUDEGAR
RUEL
RUGBY
RUGER
RULE
RUMMEL
RUNNER
RUPERT
RUPIN
RUSDAN
RUSHFORD
RUSHTON
RUSK
RUSKIN
RUSS
RUSTICE
RUSTIN
RUTHERFORD
RUTLAND
RUTLEY
RY
RYALS
RYAN
RYANDER
RYCE
RYCROFT
RYDER
RYE
RYER
RYERSON
RYKE
RYKEN
RYLAND
RYLANDER
RYLANT

RYNDOM
RYNN
RYSOM
RYSTON
RYTON
RYVERS

S

SADLER
SAE
SAGEAL
SAGER
SAI
SAIL
SAILEN
SAILOR
SAINT
SAL
SALEM
SALEN
SALFORD
SALM
SALMAN
SALTER
SALVADOR
SAM
SAMMIE
SAMSON
SANDBER
SANDER
SANDERS
SANDLER
SANDS
SANGER
SANSON
SANTIAGO
SANTINO
SANTON
SANTOSH
SASSON
SATCHEL

SATCHETT
SAUL
SAULTER
SAUNDERS
SAVAGE
SAVILLE
SAVINE
SAVIOR
SAVYON
SAWYER
SAXE
SAXON
SAXTON
SAYAN
SAYER
SCANT
SCHAFFIELD
SCHELDEN
SCHMIDT
SCHNEIDER
SCHOFIELD
SCHULER
SCHULTZ
SCHUYLEY
SCOUT
SCULLEY
SCYLER
SEABRROK
SEABURY
SEALE
SEALEY
SEARCY
SEARGEANT
SEATON
SEAVOR
SEBASTIAN
SEBRING

SEEGAR
SEELEY
SEF
SEFTON
SEGER
SELDAN
SELDON
SELLARS
SELLERS
SELVAN
SENDER
SENECA
SENNETT
SEREN
SERF
SERGE
SERGIO
SETH
SETON
SEVEN
SEVERI
SEVERN
SEVILLE
SEWARD
SEXTON
SEYMOUR
SHABAT
SHAD
SHADMAN
SHALE
SHAN
SHANAHAN
SHANCE
SHAND
SHANE
SHANKS
SHANLEY

SHANNING	SIMPSON	SMOTHER
SHAP	SIMRAN	SNEAD
SHAQ	SINGER	SNYDER
SHARIF	SIONE	SOL
SHARP	SIRAN	SOLANO
SHAW	SIRUS	SOLOMAN
SHAYDE	SIXX	SOLON
SHEDD	SKALLA	SOMERBY
SHEFFIELD	SKAY	SOMERTON
SHELBY	SKEET	SON
SHELDON	SKI	SOREL
SHELTON	SKINNER	SOREN
SHEN	SKIP	SOTHERN
SHEP	SKYLAR	SOUND
SHEPHERD	SKYLER	SOUTER
SHERMAN	SLADE	SOUTH
SHERWIN	SLADEN	SOUTHERN
SHERWOOD	SLADER	SPACEY
SHILOH	SLADON	SPALDING
SHIN	SLANE	SPARKS
SHIP	SLATE	SPARTS
SHIPLEY	SLATEN	SPAWN
SHIPTON	SLATER	SPEARS
SIAM	SLATON	SPECK
SIBLEY	SLAUGHTER	SPEEDY
SIDNEY	SLAVIN	SPEER
SIDOR	SLIDE	SPELLARS
SIDUS	SLIM	SPELLE
SIELLO	SLOAN	SPELLORS
SIGNE	SLY	SPENCE
SIKES	SLYE	SPENCER
SIL	SMEDLEY	SPERRY
SILAS	SMITH	SPIKE
SILO	SMITHERS	SPILLANE
SILVER	SMITHERSON	SPORTE
SIMM	SMITHSON	SPRINGER
SIMMS	SMITTY	SPRINTER

SPRUCE	STILLMAN	STRUTHERS
SPURLIN	STING	STRYDER
SPURS	STINGSON	STRYKER
SQUIRE	STIRLING	STRYPER
STADLER	STOCK	STUCKLER
STAM	STOCKARD	STUCKY
STAMOS	STOCKER	STYLES
STAMPER	STOCKERD	SUEDE
STANDISH	STOCKES	SUITER
STANFIELD	STOCKTON	SULLEY
STANHOPE	STOCKWELL	SULLIVAN
STANTON	STODDARD	SULLY
STARK	STODDEY	SULTAN
STARKE	STOKER	SUMIT
STARLIN	STOKES	SUMMITT
STARLING	STONE	SUMNER
STARNES	STONELIEGH	SUMTER
STASH	STONEY	SUNDER
STATLER	STOREY	SUNDERS
STATON	STRADDEN	SUNNER
STEALTH	STRATEN	SUTTER
STEDMAN	STRATFORD	SUTTON
STEED	STRATTEN	SVEN
STELLE	STRATTON	SVERE
STEIN	STRAUS	SWAIN
STEINER	STRAVOS	SWAINTON
STELLAN	STRAWDER	SWAY
STELLAR	STRICKLAND	SWIFT
STELTON	STRIDE	SWINDELL
STEN	STRIDER	SWINTON
STENT	STRIKE	SY
STERN	STROKER	SYE
STETSON	STROM	SYFRON
STEU	STROMMOND	SYGNAL
STIAN	STRUM	SYLVAN
STILES	STRUMMOND	SYMMS
STILLES	STRUMTON	SYNDAL

SYON
SYRTIS
SYRUS

T

TAB
TABOR
TACEN
TAFF
TAFT
TAGGART
TAGUE
TAHL
TAHOE
TAI
TAIR
TAIT
TAKODA
TAKOMA
TAL
TALAN
TALBIN
TALBOT
TALBOTT
TALCOTT
TALER
TALIB
TALMADGE
TALMAN
TALON
TAMER
TAMRON
TAN
TANE
TANNER
TARMY
TARVA
TASH

TASSWELL
TATE
TATUM
TAVEN
TAVEY
TAVOR
TAYDEN
TAYLON
TAYLOR
TAYSON
TAYTON
TAZ
TAZWELL
TEAGUE
TEAL
TEALE
TEDRICK
TEGAN
TEHANEY
TELEM
TELFORD
TELLER
TELM
TEMAN
TEMPLETON
TEMPY
TEM
TENDALL
TENNANT
TENNISON
TENNYSON
TENSK
TERL
TERRAN
TERRON
TET
TEVEY

TEVIN
TEX
THAD
THADD
THAI
THAINE
THALEN
THAMER
THANDE
THANE
THANN
THARPE
THATCHER
THAVIN
THEYLER
THENAN
THEO
THEON
THERMAN
THERON
THOMASON
THOMPSON
THOR
THORIN
THORN
THORNE
THORNSTON
THORPE
THORTON
THRACE
THRATCHER
THULOW
THURLON
THURLOW
THURSTON
TIBOR
TICIO

TIDE	TONIN	TRAYLOR
TIERNEY	TONY	TRAYTON
TIFTON	TOPHER	TREB
TIGER	TOPPER	TREIL
TILDAN	TOPPIN	TREND
TILDEN	TORBEN	TRENDAN
TILFORD	TORDEN	TRENNER
TILL	TORGNE	TRENT
TILLMAN	TORIAN	TRENTON
TILON	TORLESS	TREST
TILTON	TORM	TRETON
TIMBER	TORN	TREV
TIMENN	TORQ	TREVEY
TIMIN	TORR	TREVINE
TIMON	TORRENT	TREVOR
TIMUS	TORST	TREX
TINDER	TOSH	TREYSON
TINKS	TOSOAN	TRICE
TINSLEY	TOSON	TRIGG
TINSON	TOTTIVER	TRIMAN
TIPP	TOURAN	TRIMMER
TIPPERN	TOV	TRIPLER
TIPPER	TOVE	TRIPP
TIPTON	TOWNLEY	TRIPTON
TITAN	TOWNSEND	TRISTAN
TITIAN	TRACE	TRISTE
TITUS	TRACKE	TRISTRAM
TOBBY	TRAE	TRISTRAN
TOBIAS	TRAFTON	TRORRY
TOVIE	TRAIL	TROTTER
TOLA	TRAINER	TROUP
TOLBY	TRAK	TROUPER
TOLIN	TRAKE	TROUT
TOLIVER	TRAM	TRUETT
TOLOME	TRANCE	TRUMAN
TOLSON	TRAVERSE	TRUSDALE
TOLSYN	TRAVYN	TRUXTON

TRYER
TRYSTAN
TRYTON
TUCKER
TUCKS
TUFF
TULSA
TUNE
TUPPER
TURE
TURNER
TUSCAN
TUSSON
TUT
TWAIN
TWYFORD
TY
TYCE
TYE
TYEE
TYERSON
TYLER
TYLUS
TYMAN
TYNAN
TYNDAL
TYR
TYS
TYSON

U

USRY
UTAH
UTHMAN
UVINE

UAN
UBEN
UDAL
UDELL
UGO
ULAN
ULFRED
ULICK
ULLAND
ULMAN
ULRICH
ULRID
ULTAN
ULTAR
ULTON
ULYSSES
UMAR
UMBER
UNITAS
UNIVERSE
UNSEN
UNTEN
UPTON
UPWOOD
URBAN
URBAND
URIEL
URS
URSAN
URSDAN
USHER
USHTON
USMAN

V

VACHEL
VADIN
VALDETH
VALIN
VALLEN
VALOR
VALTEN
VANCE
VANDEN
VANDER
VANE
VANLEER
VANN
VANSANT
VARDEN
VARLEN
VARNA
VARNELL
VARNER
VAS
VASANT
VASCH
VASH
VASIN
VASKEN
VAUGHN
VEEJAY
VEER
VEILAN
VEILAND
VELAND
VENCE
VEND

VENDER
VENDON
VENN
VENTURE
VERAINE
VERDE
VERDELLE
VERED
VICK
VICKEN
VICKENS
VICKERS
VICTEN
VICTOR
VID
VIDOR
VILLARD
VILLEN
VIN
VINCE
VINSON
VINTON
VIPER
VIR
VISON
VITO
VITUS
VODIE
VOLF
VOLKAN
VOLKER
VOLYA
VON
VONG
VORRIS
VULCAN
VURL

W

WADE
WADEN
WAEL
WAGNER
WAGON
WAIN
WAINWRIGHT
WAIT
WAITE
WAKER
WAL
WALDEN
WALDO
WALDRON
WALES
WALFORD
WALKER
WALLER
WALLY
WALMOND
WALSH
WALTON
WARD
WARDEN
WARDLEY
WARE
WARK
WARLEY
WARNER
WARRANT
WARREN
WARTON
WASHINGTON

WATERS
WATFORD
WATKINS
WATSON
WAVES
WAYLON
WAYMOND
WAYNARD
WEAVER
WEBB
WEBBER
WEBSTER
WEISS
WELBY
WELCH
WELD
WELDOM
WELDON
WELFORD
WELLS
WELSH
WELTON
WENDELL
WENFORD
WENT
WENTWORTH
WENTZ
WENWORTH
WELEY
WERNER
WERTHER
WES
WEST
WESTCOTT
WESTER
WESTERN
WESTLEY

WESTON
WETHER
WEX
WHARTON
WHATERS
WHATLEY
WHEAT
WHEATLEY
WHEATON
WHEELER
WHIDDON
WHIT
WHITAKER
WHITBY
WHITE
WHITEY
WHITFIELD
WHITFORD
WHITMAN
WHITMORE
WHITSON
WHITTAKER
WHITTEN
WHITTIER
WHORTON
WICK
WIERHRS
WIER
WIGGINS
WILDE
WILDER
WILDES
WILDON
WILEN
WILES
WILEY
WILKES

WILKINSON WOODES WYTHE
WILL WOODFIN WYTON
WILLS WOODROW WYZE
WILSON WOODRUFF
WILT WOODSON
WILTON WOODWARD
WILTSON WOODY
WIND WORD
WINDELL WORDEN
WINDER WORDSWORTH
WINDFREY WORSH
WINDSOR WORTH
WINDWARD WORTHINGTON
WINFIELD WRAE
WINFREY WRANDI
WINGATE WRAY
WINN WREN
WINSLOW WRIGHT
WINSOME WRIGLEY
WINSTON WRISTON
WINSTONE WRY
WINTON WRYE
WINWARD WULF
WIRED WYAM
WIREN WYAN
WISHUM WYCK
WITHERS WYCLEFF
WITT WYCLIFF
WIZE WYLAND
WOHN WYLDER
WOLF WYLER
WOLFE WYMAN
WOLFIN WYMER
WOLSH WYNDHAM
WOLTER WYNTON
WOOD WYSE
WOODARD WYSTAN

X

XAN
XANDER
XANN
XAVER
XAVIER
XAXON
XEN
XENOM
XERES
XIMEN
XYLAND
XYLE
XYST
XYSTUM

Y

YADON
YAEL
YAIR
YALEN
YALES
YALMAN
YAMEN
YAN
YANCE
YANCEY
YANIS
YANN
YAO
YARDEN
YARDLEY
YARED
YAREN
YAROM
YATCH
YEARDLEY
YEATS
YEB
YELLOT
YEN
YEOMAN
YERED
YEREL
YIANNI
YIMER
YIRON
YOHAN
YORAN
YORKE
YOUNGES
YONGERS
YOVAN
YUKE
YUKON
YUL
YURI
YVES
YVONN

Z

ZAC
ZACE
ZACKERY
ZADDOX
ZADE
ZADEN
ZADOCK
ZAINE
ZALE
ZALES
ZALMAN
ZANCEY
ZANDERS
ZANE
ZANN
ZARED
ZARIN
ZAYDON
ZAYN
ZEB
ZEBUL
ZEE
ZEKE
ZELL
ZEN
ZENON
ZEPH
ZOOK
ZORAN
ZOWIE
ZOY
ZUAD
ZUBA

ZUBREN
ZUCKER
ZUMA
ZUREN
ZURY
ZYA
ZYAN
ZYKE
ZYLAN
ZYLAND
ZYLER
ZYREE